Fall on Your Knees

Fall on Your Knees

Activities and Prayer Services for Youth

Eric J. Sova

GIA Publications, Inc.
Chicago

G-6093
Copyright © 2005 GIA Publications, Inc.
7404 S. Mason Avenue, Chicago, IL 60638
www.giamusic.com
ISBN: 1-57999-530-6

Saint Joseph Edition of The New American Bible
(Catholic Book Publishing Co.: New York)

Layout and cover design: Robert M. Sacha

All rights reserved.
Printed in the United States of America.

For Jen,
the love of my life and my best friend.

Table of Contents

Part 1 – The Activities

Remember Me . . . . .Track 2 3
   Activity One: Leader Page 4
   Activity One: Student Page 6
   Activity Two: Leader Page 8
   Activity Two: Student Page 10

Reflect the Light . . . . .Track 3 13
   Activity One: Leader Page 14
   Activity One: Student Page 16
   Activity Two: Leader Page 18
   Activity Two: Student Page 20

Fall (on Your Knees) . . . . .Track 4 23
   Activity One: Leader Page 24
   Activity One: Student Page 26
   Activity Two: Leader Page 28
   Activity Two: Student Page 30

Stand Up . . . . .Track 5 33
   Activity One: Leader Page 34
   Activity One: Student Page 36
   Activity Two: Leader Page 38
   Activity Two: Student Page 40

Site for Sore Eyes . . . . .Track 6 43
   Activity One: Leader Page 44
   Activity One: Student Page 46
   Activity Two: Leader Page 50
   Activity Two: Student Page 52

His Life . . . . .Track 7 55
   Activity One: Leader Page 56
   Activity One: Student Page 58
   Activity Two: Leader Page 60
   Activity Two: Student Page 62

Wish . . . . .Track 8 65
    Activity One: Leader Page 66
    Activity One: Student Page 68
    Activity Two: Leader Page 70
    Activity Two: Student Page 72

Praise . . . . .Track 9 75
    Activity One: Leader Page 76
    Activity One: Student Page 78
    Activity Two: Leader Page 80
    Activity Two: Student Page 82

Nails That Pierced . . . . .Track 10 85
    Activity One: Leader Page 86
    Activity One: Student Page 88
    Activity Two: Leader Page 98
    Activity Two: Student Page 100

This Is Your Choice . . . . .Track 11 103
    Activity One: Leader Page 104
    Activity One: Student Page 106
    Activity Two: Leader Page 109
    Activity Two: Student Page 114

Part 2 – The Prayer Services

Remember Me . . . . .Track 2 119
Reflect the Light . . . . .Track 3 123
Fall (on Your Knees) . . . . .Track 4 125
Stand Up . . . . .Track 5 129
Site for Sore Eyes . . . . .Track 6 133
His Life . . . . .Track 7 137
Wish . . . . .Track 8 141
Praise . . . . .Track 9 145
Nails That Pierced . . . . .Track 10 149
This Is Your Choice . . . . .Track 11 155

Preface

The most common challenge over my years in youth ministry can be summed up in one word: programming. On more than one occasion, creating an interesting as well as faith-building program for my group became very frustrating. There were other times when I would need to plan a prayer service in a matter of minutes, sometimes with success and other times without. Most youth ministers I know have been in a similar position at one time or another—hence, the purpose of this book.

In this book you will find 20 activities and 10 prayer services centered around the music on my *Fall on Your Knees* CD. Each activity strives to engage young people in the Gospel message of Christ, utilizing music as a tool to reach the youth culture. This resource is designed for the seasoned youth minister as well as the part-time weekly volunteer. Each session provides both a **leader page** and a **student page**, with step-by-step instructions to make the program successful. You may choose to follow each step as written, or you might want to customize any of the activities for your particular group. I believe flexibility is important in creating dynamic youth ministry programming.

Whether you are new to youth ministry or have been working with young people for many years, this resource will be a valuable tool in conquering the challenge of programming.

May God bless your work with the youth of the Church.

—*Eric J. Sova*

Part 1
The Activities

Remember Me

Written by Eric J. Sova and Joseph Mills

Lyrics

The Lord is my shepherd there is nothing I shall want. He lets me rest in the fields of green and he leads me to his font. He gives me all the strength I need as he guides me down my path. If I travel through the darkest valleys he protects me with his staff.

So remember me in your kingdom, Lord. Remember me, O Lord. Won't you remember me in my darkest hour? Remember me, O Lord.

You spread your table before me in the sight of all my foes. You anoint my head with your holy oil and my cup overflows.

Only goodness and kindness follow me, all the days of my life. And I shall dwell in the house of the Lord, for eternity. Won't you remember me? Remember me.

So remember me in your kingdom, Lord. Remember me, O Lord. Won't you remember me in my darkest hour? Remember me, O Lord. Won't you remember me? Will you remember me?

Song Background

I originally wrote this song for a funeral of a family member. The lyrics were taken directly from Psalm 23 and the music was very mellow. When we sat down to record for the CD, we decided to rewrite the music to make the song much more powerful. This was necessary because, within these words, we can put every confidence in Christ to protect and watch over us.

Related Scripture

Psalm 23
Luke 23:40–43
2 Corinthians 1:3–10

Activities

Activity One
Leader Page

Written by Eric J. Sova and Joseph Mills

Activity Theme
Use this song to plan a discussion activity around who Christ is to us and how we trust in the Lord.

Preparation
You will need the following items for this activity:
- Bibles for each student (or have them share)
- String or yarn (enough for approximately 5 feet per student)
- Index cards (1 per student)
- Writing utensil (1 per student)
- Copy of Student Page (for each participant)

Opening Prayer
Begin the session by asking a student leader or an adult to lead the group in prayer. Focus of the prayer should be based on opening everyone's heart and mind to allow Christ's teachings that are present within this activity to enter their lives.

Opening Activity
Give each student a copy of the Student Page and a writing utensil. Ask the students to listen to the song "Remember Me" while following along with the lyrics. After the song has played, have the students write down answers to the General Questions on the Student Page.

Play the song again while the students are working. Once the students are done with the questions, have them gather in groups of 6 to 8 and share any 3 of their answers with each other. When finished, have them look up Psalm 23 and Luke 23:40–43, and answer the Scripture Questions on the Student Page.

Testimonial
Ask one or two students to share a short story of a time in their life when they believe Christ had "remembered" them. If having two students share, ask one to share of a trying time in his or her life ("their darkest hour") and the other to share of a very joyful time ("spread his table before them").

Reflection

Give each student a piece of string or yarn. Ask them to close their eyes and reflect upon the previous week and/or month—what it was like at school, at home, at work, or out with their friends. Have them picture in their minds the good times they had as well as the troubled times. For each memory, have them tie a knot in the string approximately 6 inches apart.

Activity

Give each student an index card. Ask them to write down 4 words that describe Jesus Christ in their life. Stimulate ideas by giving examples like "Savior" and "teacher." Next to each of the 4 words the students wrote, have them list someone in their life who fits these roles/words. Once finished, use a hole punch or tape to connect the cards to their string of knots. Next, have students complete the Final Activity on the Student Page.

Challenge

During every day of the next week, ask the students to spend time in prayer with their string of knots. Have them visualize each of the events the knots represent. A "Hail Mary" or "Glory Be" should be said with each knot. Also have them thank God for the blessings of the people who are Christ to them in their daily lives.

Activities

Activity One
Student Page

Remember Me

Written by Eric J. Sova and Joseph Mills

Opening Activity

After listening to the song, answer the following 4 questions as best as you can. You may be asked to share your answers.

1. What are the different roles that Jesus fulfills for the writer?

   _____
   _____
   _____

2. How does this song relate to your life as a teen?

   _____
   _____
   _____

3. Explain one situation in your life when Jesus was a "shepherd" to you.

   _____
   _____
   _____

4. In what kinds of situations can you rely on Jesus to give you strength and guidance?

   _____
   _____
   _____

Reflection

Only answer these questions after you have read the suggested readings.

Suggested Reading: Psalm 23

1. What does this Psalm tell you about how you should live your life?

   _____
   _____
   _____

2. What does our Catholic faith teach us about Christ's love for us? Are there any situations we could be in when Christ would not give us his love?

_____
_____
_____

3. Would Christ ever not "remember us"? Why or why not?

_____
_____
_____

Suggested Reading: Luke 23:40–43

1. How would you describe the courage and faith of the two criminals? How do they differ?

_____
_____
_____

2. What situations in your life relate to the first criminal? The second criminal?

_____
_____
_____

Activity

Do not complete this section until instructed to do so.

Take the string and tie the loose ends together. Keep the string in a safe place throughout the next couple of weeks. It is a symbol of Christ's never-ending love. Each of the events knotted in this string is tied to the love of Christ.

Look at each of the knots. Notice that they do not break the string but rather wrap the string. This is the same with Christ's love. The events that the knots represent do not break the bond of Christ's love, but instead they are wrapped tightly in his love.

Challenge

Your challenge this week is to daily spend time in prayer with your string of knots. Visualize each of the events the knots represent. Say a "Hail Mary" or "Glory Be" with each knot. Also thank God for the blessings of the people who are Christ to you in your daily lives.

During your challenge this week, visualize the love of Christ wrapped around your life. Remember to give thanks in your prayers.

Activities

Activity Two
Leader Page

Remember Me

Written by Eric J. Sova and Joseph Mills

Activity Theme Students deal with many different types of crises in their lives. Some of these are within their families, between their peers, or even within themselves. These crises vary with every situation. Use this activity and song to examine how students deal with the crises in their lives.

Preparation You will need the following items for this activity:
- Bibles for each student (or have them share)
- 6-inch square (approximate) pieces of torn brown paper bag (1 per student)
- Writing utensil (one per student)
- Crayons or markers (several per student)
- Piece of newsprint paper (1 per 3 students)
- Copy of Student Page (for each participant)

Opening Prayer Begin the session by asking a student leader or an adult to lead the group in prayer. Focus the prayer around the words of 2 Corinthians 1:3–10, especially verses 4 and 10.

Opening Activity Give each student a copy of the Student Page, the piece of brown paper bag, and a writing utensil. Split the students into groups of 3 and have them write down 5 different types of crises that teens routinely go through. When they are finished identifying their 5 crises, have them choose the 3 most difficult and write those on separate pieces of paper bag. When finished, collect all of the bag pieces. These will be redistributed after the testimonials.

Testimonial Ask one or two students to share a short story of a time in their life when they relied on Christ to get them through a crisis. You will want to preview these testimonials prior to having your students present them. The purpose of the testimonial is to share a message of Christ's love and compassion for us—it is not a competition to see who can tell the saddest story. Be sure to encourage the students to give a brief background of the crisis and to freely elaborate on how Christ helped them.

Reflection

Randomly redistribute the pieces of brown paper bag. Ask the students to visualize themselves in a situation like that which is written on the paper. Ask them to think about answers to the following 3 questions:

1. What would you do if you were in this situation?
2. How would you react to the crisis?
3. What role would your faith play in the healing process?

After a few moments of silence, ask the students to think about their answers, play the song "Remember Me," and ask the students to follow along with the lyrics.

Activity

Have students return to their original groups of three. Give each group a piece of newsprint and several markers or crayons. Have each group choose one of the crises they randomly received. On the newsprint, have the students create an advertisement that promotes their faith and belief in God as a solution for the chosen crisis. They can choose their main theme for the ad from either the song or the scripture reading from 2 Corinthians. When finished, display the advertisements on a wall for everyone to see.

Challenge

During every day of the next week, ask the students to spend time in prayer with their piece of brown paper bag. Have them pray for all people who suffer through the crisis that is written on their paper. Especially have them remember friends, family members, or acquaintances who are currently suffering through their crisis.

Activities

Activity Two
Student Page

Remember Me

Written by Eric J. Sova and Joseph Mills

Opening Activity Take a moment to think of different types of crises that teens routinely go through. These could happen at school, at home, or at work. List the 5 crises you think happen the most often.

1. _____
2. _____
3. _____
4. _____
5. _____

Then answer the following 2 questions:

1. Why did you choose these 5 crises?

   _____
   _____
   _____

2. Do you know anyone who is currently in one of these situations?

   _____
   _____
   _____

Rank the above crises in order of severity. Choose the 3 greatest and write them on the different pieces of brown paper.

Reflection

You have randomly been given one of the crises the group has identified. Take a moment to visualize what it would be like if you were in this situation. Think of someone you know who might be going through this right now. Answer the following 3 questions in your mind:

1. What would you do if you were in this situation?
2. How would you react to the crisis?
3. What role would your faith play in the healing process?

The song "Remember Me" talks about Jesus as our shepherd. He protects us and cares for us. We ask him to remember us in our good times and our bad times. How does this song relate to recovering from the crises we face in our day-to-day lives?

Activity

Your group has been given a piece of newsprint paper. On this paper you are to create an advertisement that promotes your faith and belief in God as a solution for one of the group's crises. Use the scripture reading from the Opening Prayer or the lyrics from the song "Remember Me" to help you create a theme for your advertisement. You might want to develop a slogan or some other catchy phrase that would draw attention to your theme.

Challenge

Your challenge this week is to daily review the crisis on your piece of brown paper. While thinking about the crisis, take time to remember in prayer all of those people who are currently suffering because of a related situation. We pray that Christ will remember us, but we must also remember in our prayers those who suffer.

Reflect the Light

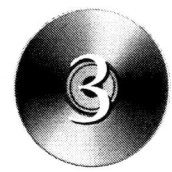

Activities

Written by Eric J. Sova

Lyrics

There's a light in the darkness, that the world needs to see. That a man named Jesus, had come to set us free. There's a light in the darkness, that's held within your soul. It remains just a whisper, until your heart begins to grow.

When you reflect the light, it consumes your life and your love begins to shine. For the call of faith will lead you to his love. When you reflect the light, it consumes the lives of the friends you call your own. For the light of faith will burn in their souls. When you reflect the light.

There's a light in the darkness, that glows in your hand. You are called by the Father, to share it with the land. There's a light in the darkness, that sparkles in your eyes. With a shimmer of freedom, you have given him your life.

The struggles will be real, and your light will seem to fade. If you hold on to his love, your light will shine on faith.

Song Background

I have always been inspired by the fact that Christ is the light of the world and that as his followers we, too, can be lights for others who are lost in the darkness and confusion of life. This song highlights my inspiration. We are called as Christians to be witnesses for Christ. Through our witnessing, we have the opportunity to live the message of this song—to reflect the light.

Related Scripture

Matthew 5:14–16
John 3:16–21
John 1:4–9
2 Corinthians 4:1–6

Activities

Activity One
Leader Page

Reflect the Light

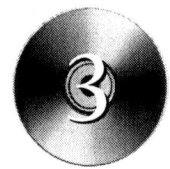

Written by Eric J. Sova

Activity Theme

Students have a unique ability and a responsibility to be the light for their peers. This event will focus on being that light and living the call to witness.

Preparation

You will need the following items for this activity:
- Bibles for each student (or have them share)
- Candle and matches or a lighter
- Votive candles (1 per student)
- Writing utensil (1 per student)
- Copy of Student Page (for each participant)

Opening Prayer

Begin the session by having all students sit in a circle. Turn out all the lights so the room is completely dark. If needed, cover any miscellaneous sources of light. Place an unlit candle in the center of the room. With all of the lights out, recite Genesis 1:1–5. Pause for approximately 10 seconds and then light the candle in the center of the room.

Have an adult leader read the following statement to the students:

> When God created the world, he separated us from the darkness. When God gave us his Son, he gave us a person to follow out of darkness. When God called us to be his disciples, he called us to lead others out of darkness. This candle, as small as it is in this large room, has broken the darkness that surrounded us. We, too, can break the darkness that surrounds those we come in contact with throughout our lives. Stare at the flame. Notice the intensity of something so small. Concentrate on the flame as you listen to these words.

Then play the song "Reflect the Light" while the students sit in silence staring at the candle.

Activities

Opening Activity — Give each student a copy of the Student Page and a writing utensil. Have the students do the Opening Activity in pairs.

Testimonial — Ask one of the students to share a short testimonial about a time in his or her life when he or she became the light for a friend or family member who was struggling with their faith. Have the students explain how they were a light for others and how it made them feel afterwards.

Reflection — Have each student reread the lyrics to the song. Ask them to reflect on the areas of their life where they could spread the light of Christ. Then have them create a list on the Student Page.

Activity — If the appropriate resources are available, you might consider having the students make their own candles instead of giving them votive candles. Be sure to try this on your own first so you have a little practice. Another option would be to have the adults and other student leaders meet before the event to make the candles for the rest of the group.

Challenge — Give each student a votive candle to take home with them. Ask the students to light the candle during their nightly prayers so it reminds them to become the light of Christ. (Remind the students to be careful with fire. For younger students, this challenge might be better suited as a nightly family event.)

Activities

Activity One
Student Page

Reflect the Light

Written by Eric J. Sova

Opening Activity

Look up and read Matthew 5:14–16, John 3:16–21, John 1:4–9, and 2 Corinthians 4:1–6. When finished, answer the following questions by yourself and then share your answers with your partner.

1. How does each of these scripture readings tell us about how we should live our lives?

   _____
   _____
   _____

2. What kinds of things make it difficult for a teenager to live the life that reflects Christ's light?

   _____
   _____
   _____

3. What can a young person do to make reflecting Christ's light easier?

   _____
   _____
   _____

4. Write down 3 names of people who would support you in your journey to become a light of Christ.

   a. _____

   b. _____

   c. _____

5. Explain to your partner why you chose these people.

_____
_____
_____

Reflection Do not complete this section until instructed to do so.

After rereading the words to the song "Reflect the Light," create a list of activities, events, people, etc., in your life who you feel you could spread the light of Christ to.

_____
_____
_____
_____
_____
_____
_____
_____

Activity and Challenge Do not complete this section until instructed to do so.

Today we have spent a lot of time on how we should become the light of Christ for our family and friends. Write a short prayer you can recite nightly during the week asking God for assistance in accomplishing the items on the list you wrote during the Reflection.

Activities

Activity Two
Leader Page

Reflect the Light

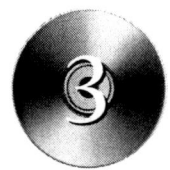

Written by Eric J. Sova

Activity Theme

We are constantly called by God to live a life representative of Christ. When we answer this call, we are consumed by God's love. Then in turn, we reflect that love to others. This activity provides an opportunity for young people to discover God's call within themselves.

Preparation

You will need the following items for this discussion:
- Bibles for each student (or have them share)
- Several large mirrors
- Writing utensil (one per student)
- Permanent markers (at least 1 per 3 students)
- Aluminum foil (enough for 1 square foot per student)
- Copy of Student Page (for each participant)

Set the mirrors up against the wall in the front of the room to enable the students to see themselves throughout most of the activity and discussions.

Opening Prayer

Begin the session by asking all of the students to sit in a position so they can see their reflection in at least one of the mirrors. Then have an adult or a student leader read the following prayer:

> Heavenly Father, thank you for bringing us together to share in this time of learning. We ask that you open our hearts and our minds that we may more fully understand how we can become reflections of your love. Be with us as we share, and help us to carry the lessons we learn today into our everyday lives.
>
> We ask this in the name of our Lord, Jesus Christ.
>
> Amen.

Fall on Your Knees · Reflect the Light

Opening Activity Give each student a copy of the Student Page and ask them to complete the opening activity. When finished, ask them to share their pictures in groups of 6 or 8.

Testimonial Ask one of the students to share a short story about a time in his or her life when he or she felt challenged to live a life that was representative of Christ. Be sure students include the rewards and gifts received from reflecting Christ's love.

Reflection After they have shared their pictures with each other, have the students gather in front of the mirrors again. Make sure students can see their own reflection, and then play the song "Reflect the Light." Have the students follow along with the lyrics of the song as it is played. Then ask them to complete the Reflection section of the Student Page. If you would like, replay the song as the students are working on the activity.

Challenge Give each student a piece of aluminum foil and a permanent marker (or have them share the marker). Have each of the students write the answer, or a brief description, to the last question of the Reflection activity on the aluminum foil. Then have them fold the foil until it is about the size of a business card. The challenge for the students is to carry this piece of foil around with them all week long. Every time they reach into their pocket, they should say a quick prayer asking God to help them improve themselves. With prayer and commitment, they will reflect the light of Christ in their daily lives.

Activities

Activities

Activity Two
Student Page

Reflect the Light

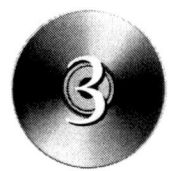

Written by Eric J. Sova

Opening Activity In each of the 4 boxes below, draw a picture that represents the phrase inside the box. You may not use words or letters—just images.

My Personality

My Strengths

My Weaknesses

My Faith

Reflection

Do not complete this section until instructed to do so.

Follow along to the lyrics of the song "Reflect the Light." Think about your 4 drawings and how they fit into the words from this song. Then in the space provided below, write down the first thought that comes to mind as you stare into your reflection and answer the following 4 questions:

1. What do you see?
   _____
   _____
   _____

2. How accurate were you with your 4 drawings above? Why or why not?
   _____
   _____
   _____

3. How do you reflect the light of Christ?
   _____
   _____
   _____

4. What can you improve upon?
   _____
   _____
   _____

Challenge

Do not complete this section until instructed to do so.

You have been given a piece of aluminum foil and a marker. Write the answer to the last question from the Reflection above on your foil. Now fold the foil up until it is about the size of a business card. Your challenge this week is to carry this foil with you everywhere you go. Whenever you reach into your pocket, you will be reminded of your answer. At that time, take a moment and pray that God will help you improve your ability to reflect the light of Christ in your daily life.

Fall (On Your Knees)

Written by Eric J. Sova

Lyrics

On Sundays you come to the church, to listen to his holy word. Do you leave it right there in the chair as you leave, or do you take what you learn to the world? You come to the table to eat, to share in the gift of the lamb. Do you truly believe that it's Christ in your palm or do you think that it's bread in your hand?

Do you fall on your knees when the world knocks you down? Do you run from the God whom you fear? Do you lose all your faith when your friends cut it down? Do you know he is near? Do you know Christ is here?

You choose how to live every day and stumble and fall along the way. Do you think you can wait before you change your heart, or do you walk in his footsteps today?

Song Background

This song touches on so many subjects that relate to our Catholic faith. It challenges us to look at how we practice our faith. I think it is so important for teens today to ask themselves the very questions presented in this song. Do we fall on our knees? Do we run? Do we lose all our faith? Or do we believe?

Related Scripture

John 6:32–37
Mark 14:22–25
James 5:13–18

Activities

Activity One
Leader Page

Fall (On Your Knees)

Written by Eric J. Sova

Activity Theme
Every Catholic Christian struggles with their faith at one time or another. This activity focuses on how we live our Catholic identity in worship and in the practice of our Sacraments.

Preparation
You will need the following items for this activity:
- Bibles for each student (or have them share)
- Newsprint or poster paper (hung on the wall in the front of the room)
- Writing utensil (1 per student)
- Copy of Student Page (for each participant)

Opening Prayer
Begin the session by asking a student leader or an adult to lead the group in a prayer focused around praying for those who struggle with their faith. This might also include prayers asking the Holy Spirit to assist the group in their journey of faith.

Opening Activity
Take all the students into church and have them sit for 5 minutes. Do not plan anything—just have them sit there. Then bring them back into your gathering space. Give each student a copy of the Student Page and a writing utensil. Have them complete the Opening Activity questions on the Student Page on their own. Then hold a short discussion on the answers they wrote down. The students most likely will not have any answers that really have a point. (Some might.)

Relate their experience in the church to what it is like if they just simply go to church on Sunday and not participate. Then list the different parts of the mass; explain what we receive at each part and what we can learn from each part. For example, during the scripture readings we listen to the Word of God and must think about how it affects and applies to our lives. Even though the Bible was written many years ago, there are great lessons to learn, but we must listen if we are to learn. Another example would be the homily. It serves many roles, but primarily it provides a time for the priest or deacon to teach the members of the faith community about many things like the scripture readings of the day or church history and traditions.

Testimonial   Ask a student to share a short testimonial about why he or she practices the Sacraments. Have students explain why they think it is especially important for teenagers to actively participate in the Sacraments of the Catholic faith.

Reflection   Play the song "Fall (On Your Knees)." Separate the students into groups of 4. Ask different groups to concentrate on the first or second verse of the song and then another group to concentrate on the chorus. Have them answer the Reflection questions on the Student Page. When they are finished answering the questions, have them write their lists from the last question on the newsprint that you have hung on the wall in the front of the room.

Challenge   Ask the students to spend at least 4 nights over the next week looking up the suggested readings and completing the Challenge activity on the Student Page for each of the readings. You might encourage them to use this activity as their nightly prayers for the week.

Activities

Activity One
Student Page

Fall (On Your Knees)

Written by Eric J. Sova

Opening Activity

You just spent approximately 5 minutes sitting in the church. Take a moment and answer the following 4 questions:

1. What did you learn from your experience?
   _____
   _____

2. How will today's church experience change the way you live your life?
   _____
   _____

3. How important do you think it was that you spent time at church today?
   _____
   _____

4. Imagine doing this every week. What would you learn then?
   _____
   _____

Reflection

Do not complete this section until instructed to do so.

After listening to the song "Fall (On Your Knees)," you will be assigned a verse or the chorus. Answer the following 3 questions as they relate to your assigned section of the song:

1. What do you feel is the primary message in this section of the song?
   _____
   _____

2. How does this apply to your life as a teenager?

   _____
   _____

3. List 3 changes you could make in your daily life that would allow you to answer the call of this song?

   a. _____
      _____

   b. _____
      _____

   c. _____
      _____

Activity and Challenge

Select 4 nights over the next week. For each of the nights, select one of the suggested readings. During your nightly prayers, take time to read the selected scripture. When you are done, think and pray about the following questions.

1. What lesson or lessons are held within this scripture reading?

   _____
   _____
   _____

2. If you had to explain this scripture verse to a friend, what would you say?

   _____
   _____
   _____

When finished and before going to bed, pray this prayer:

> Heavenly Father, thank you for all the gifts you give to me. Please help me to understand and learn from your holy words. Bless my week and bless all those I may come in contact with.
>
> I ask this in your name, my Lord, Jesus Christ.
>
> Amen.

Activities

Activity Two
Leader Page

Fall (On Your Knees)

Written by Eric J. Sova

Activity Theme The Eucharist is the centerpiece of the Catholic faith. Use this activity to highlight the importance of understanding the sacredness and the true presence of Christ in the Eucharist.

Preparation You will need the following items for this activity:
- Bibles for each student (or have them share)
- Small sheets of scratch paper (1 per student)
- Writing utensil (1 per student)
- Table and tablecloth
- Bowl with unconsecrated hosts
- Glass of wine
- Copy of Eucharistic Prayer II (1 per participant)
- Copy of Student Page (for each participant)

Set up the table in the front of the room with hosts and wine sitting in the middle. You might also light 2 candles on either side of the table.

Opening Prayer Have a student leader or an adult lead the group in a prayer that focuses on forming a personal relationship with Jesus Christ. This prayer should also include thanksgiving for the blessings received from God.

Opening Activity Give each student a copy of the Student Page and ask them to complete the Opening Activity questions. These questions focus on what the students can see on the table with the bread and wine.

Presentation Ask your pastor, a deacon, or a lay person to come in to give a short presentation on the Eucharist. The main focus for the presentation should be on the fact that Christ is truly present within the Eucharist and, as young people, we must accept this mystery based on our faith. The presenter should also address the sacredness of the Body of Christ. A tour of the church might also be appropriate to show students where the consecrated Eucharist is stored if it is not consumed during a mass and why this is important.

Testimonial Ask a student leader or an adult who regularly goes to Eucharistic Adoration to share about their experiences. It is important for us as Catholics that we find the true presence of Christ within the Eucharist. Adoration allows us to prayerfully come "face to face" with Christ's presence. It also allows us to realize that Christ is a true person for us to go to at all times, whether good or bad. Most young people do not know much about Eucharistic Adoration, so it is important that your presenter can explain the who, what, how, and why with a positive and encouraging attitude.

Reflection Play the song "Fall (On Your Knees)" and ask the students to complete the Reflection questions with a partner. When finished, present every student with a copy of the Eucharistic Prayer II.

Challenge Challenge the students to read through the Eucharistic Prayer each night before they go to bed. After they have read through it, encourage them to pray for a greater understanding of the gift that Christ has given us through the Eucharist.

Activities

Activity Two
Student Page

Fall (On Your Knees)

Written by Eric J. Sova

Opening Activity

The Eucharist is the centerpiece of our Catholic faith. We are given the opportunity to form a personal relationship with Christ through the gift of his body and blood. Take a moment and look at the table that is before you. Think about what you see. Think about what each of these items symbolize and answer the following 5 questions:

1. What is the importance of each of the items on the table? Explain each one.

   _____
   _____

2. How does each of the items on the table bring you closer to God?

   _____
   _____

3. Why do you believe that Christ is truly present in the Eucharist?

   _____
   _____

4. Is going to communion during mass important to you? Why or why not?

   _____
   _____

5. Why is the Eucharist considered a gift?

   _____
   _____

Fall on Your Knees · Fall (On Your Knees)

Activities

Presentation List 5 points the presenter mentioned about Eucharist that you would like to remember after today:

1. _____
_____

2. _____
_____

3. _____
_____

4. _____
_____

5. _____
_____

Reflection Do not complete this section until instructed to do so.

After listening to "Fall (On Your Knees)," answer the following 3 questions:

1. What does the song say about the Eucharist?
_____
_____

2. How can you as a young person live the life that the song talks about?
_____
_____

3. Read through the Eucharistic Prayer you have been given. How many different parts are there to the prayer? What does each part mean?
_____
_____

Challenge You have been given a copy of the Eucharistic Prayer II. This is the most commonly used Eucharistic Prayer. Every night this week, take some time before you go to bed and read through the Eucharistic Prayer. Think about what it is saying. After you have read through it, pray for a greater understanding of the gift that Christ has given us through the Eucharist.

Stand Up

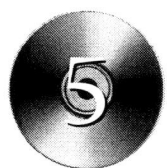

Written by Dave Lyle and Eric J. Sova

Lyrics

No one said your course in life would be a free and easy road. No one's ever handing out free rides. Sometimes it's hard to carry on beneath that heavy load. Seems like it's coming from all sides. But even in the thick of the fight, your fire inside is still burning bright.

I know how it gets sometimes, you think you're gonna lose your mind. Life's got your back against the wall. All the dreams you dare to dream will vanish in the air it seems. Wonder why you even try at all. But now is the time you must stand strong. If you trust in your faith, you can't go wrong.

Stand up right now and hear the call. If you're gonna fly, you can't be afraid to fall. Stand up and break on through it all and find your dreams.

I've been there before, my friend, I thought tough times would never end. Seemed like I was just spinning my wheels. I stood firm in that lonely place, I held on strong, I kept true faith. Now I know how real happiness feels. Cause when your dreams are falling through the floor, that's when you've got to want them even more.

If you stand up for your faith, you will have all you need. If you stand up for your faith, you'll find and know your dreams. If you stand up for your faith.

Song Background

We have so many hopes and dreams in our lives. Many times it is easy for us to get discouraged and frustrated with the difficulty that we sometimes have achieving our dreams. This song was written to express the need for us as Christians to answer the call of trusting in our faith. When we "stand up," we allow ourselves to be directed by God's will.

Related Scripture

Colossians 1:21–23
Ephesians 3:12–13
1 Samuel 3:1–10

Activities

Activity One
Leader Page

Stand Up

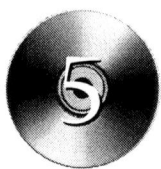

Written by Dave Lyle and Eric J. Sova

Activity Theme

This activity provides an opportunity for participants to examine how they can better their lives by trusting in their faith on a daily basis. We accomplish this by first creating images of trust and then relating those images to our faith.

Preparation

You will need the following items for this activity:
- Bibles for each student (or have them share)
- Writing utensil (1 per student)
- Old magazines from variety of sources (at least 1 per student)
- Scissors (at least 1 per pair of students)
- Scotch tape or rubber cement
- Large piece of poster board, approximately 2-foot square (1 per pair of students)
- Copy of Student Page (for each participant)

Opening Prayer

Begin the session by asking a student leader or an adult to lead the group in a prayer focused on our need to trust in our faith and for all participants to gain a better understanding of the importance of trusting in our faith.

Opening Activity

Have students gather into groups of 2. Give each student a copy of the Student Page and a writing utensil. Also give each pair at least 2 magazines, a large piece of poster board, Scotch tape or glue, and a pair of scissors.

Give the groups 15 minutes to find images inside their magazines that represent trust. Once they find these images, they are to cut them out and attach them on the poster board. Under each image, ask the students to write a brief description explaining why they feel this is an image of trust. Once this is completed, ask each pair of students to share their images with another pair of students. After they have shared their images with each other, they should complete the Opening Activity questions on the Student Page.

Testimonial Ask a student to share a short story of a time in his or her life when he or she needed to trust in God and have faith to achieve what he or she set out to do. This could be an activity in school, church, or a personal challenge the student overcame.

Reflection Play the song "Stand Up" and then ask each student to complete the Reflection questions on the Student Page.

Activity After the Reflection questions have been answered, ask the groups of pairs who originally shared their images to pick 1 of the 6 images from the group that best represents the song. This image should also represent our need as Christians to trust in our faith. Have the groups of 4 then present their image to the rest of the students. They should explain the connection to the song and our need to trust in our faith.

Challenge In the Challenge section of the Student Page, ask each student to write down 2 aspects of their life where they feel they need to trust in their faith more. Challenge each student to spend time in prayer asking for God's help in those 2 areas. You might encourage each of the pairs to pray not only for themselves but also for their partner.

Activities

Activity One
Student Page

Stand Up

Written by Dave Lyle and Eric J. Sova

Opening Activity

We must trust in our faith to achieve our hopes and our dreams. Sometimes this can be very difficult because we don't always look toward our faith for answers. In the next few minutes, you will be looking in magazines in search of 3 images that represent trust. When selecting your images, consider how your image might also represent the challenge Christians have to trust in their faith. Once you have found your 3 images, cut them out and paste them onto your poster board. Under each of the images, work with your partner to write a brief description explaining why you feel this is an image of trust. When you are finished, you will be asked to share your images with another group of students.

Do not answer the following questions until instructed to do so.

1. What kinds of things happen in our life as a direct result from trusting in our faith?

   _____

   _____

2. Why is it important for us to trust in our faith in everything that we do?

   _____

   _____

3. On a scale of 1 to 10, how much do you trust in your faith to achieve all that you want to achieve?

   _____

   _____

4. What image from the other group most represents not only the concept of trust but also the need to trust in our faith? Why?

   _____

   _____

Fall on Your Knees · Stand Up

Activities

Reflection The song "Stand Up" talks about hearing the call to stand up for your faith to achieve your dreams. There are tough times and frustrating times, but through all of it, if we trust in our faith we can achieve anything.

1. What part of this song best relates to where you feel you are at in your life today?

   _____
   _____

2. The song states, "If you're gonna fly, you can't be afraid to fall." How does this relate to the challenge of living your Christian faith on a daily basis?

   _____
   _____

3. It is hard for us to live a life that trusts completely in our faith without encouragement and support from those people around us. Who in your life can you turn to for that support?

   _____
   _____

Activity Get back together with the other group of students you were with a few minutes ago. Of the 6 images of trust you have found, choose one that best represents the song "Stand Up" and also our need as Christians to trust in our faith. Cut out that image and description. In a few minutes, you will be asked to present your image to the rest of the students.

Challenge List 2 areas of your life where you feel you need to trust in your faith more:

1. _____
   _____

2. _____
   _____

Over the next week, include these 2 areas in your nightly prayers. Ask God to assist you in furthering your relationship with him by trusting more in your faith as you encounter challenges in your daily life.

Activities

Activity Two
Leader Page

Stand Up

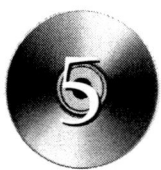

Written by Dave Lyle and Eric J. Sova

Activity Theme — As Catholic Christians, we are all called to protect the faith. This activity will focus on the need for young people to take the responsibility to stand up for their faith in their daily lives. It will also focus on the need for teens to set the example in all that they do.

Preparation — You will need the following items for this activity:
- Bibles for each student (or have them share)
- Writing utensil (1 per student)
- Several decks of playing cards (enough for at least 1 card per student)
- Large pieces of paper (4)
- Copy of Student Page (for each participant)

Opening Prayer — Ask a student leader or an adult to lead the group in a prayer that focuses on committing ourselves to our faith. The prayer should address the challenges we have when people question us about our faith and when they put us down for believing in God. The prayer should also pray for all those who suffer persecution because of their faith.

Opening Activity — Give each student a copy of the Student Page, and have the students gather into groups of four. Ask each student to briefly answer the Opening Activity questions and then share their answers with their small group.

Testimonial — Ask a student leader or an adult to share a short testimonial about a time in the student's life when he or she had to defend his or her faith. Ask them to share their fears and their rewards for standing up for what they believe.

Reflection — Play the song "Stand Up." Ask the students to follow along with the lyrics as the song is played. Then ask them to answer the Reflection questions on the Student Page.

Activity When the students are finished with the questions, discard all of the jokers from the playing cards and then give each student 1 card. Ask the students to gather into the 4 different suits (i.e., hearts, clubs, spades, and diamonds). Once in their groups, have the groups create a list of prayer intentions for each type of card. These prayer intentions should focus on the challenges that each of us has when our faith is challenged by someone else. (For example: Aces – Pray for strength to stand up to ridicule when people tease me about going to church.) Once all of the cards have been assigned a prayer intention, have a member of the group write down each card and the appropriate intention on the large sheet of paper.

Challenge Encourage each of the students to spend time in prayer this week remembering all of the intentions they created for their suit of cards. Also, challenge the students to carry their personal card with them all week long and pray especially for their particular prayer intention represented by their card.

Activity Two
Student Page

Stand Up

Written by Dave Lyle and Eric J. Sova

Opening Activity

Answer the following 2 questions, and then share your answers with the other students in your small group.

1. Briefly explain a time in your life when someone has challenged you to explain something about your faith. How did you feel? How did you explain it?

   _____
   _____
   _____

2. Do you find it difficult to stand up for what you believe in when your friends act like your beliefs are unimportant? Why?

   _____
   _____
   _____

Reflection

Do not complete this section until instructed to do so.

After listening to the song "Stand Up," answer the following 3 questions:

1. The song talks about "If you're gonna fly you can't be afraid to fall." How does this relate to defending your faith?

   _____
   _____
   _____

2. Many Christians throughout history have lost their lives because they would not turn away from their faith. What parts of the song relate to their commitment to faith?

   _____
   _____
   _____

3. What are the "dreams" we will find if we stand up for our faith?

_____
_____
_____

Activity You have been given a playing card and asked to gather into groups of a common suit (i.e., hearts, clubs, spades, and diamonds). Create a list of prayer intentions for each type of card that focuses on the challenges each of us have when our faith is challenged by someone. (For example: Aces – Pray for strength to stand up to ridicule when people tease me about going to church.) Once all of the cards have been assigned a prayer intention, have a member of your group write down each card and the appropriate intention on the large sheet of paper.

Challenge Carry your card with you all week long. Take time every day to pray for your particular prayer intention that is represented by your card. Every evening, remember in prayer all of the intentions your group created for your suit of cards.

Site for Sore Eyes

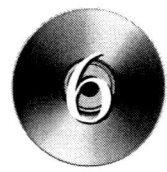

Written by Eric J. Sova

Lyrics

If you're looking for Jesus tonight, you will find him in your sight. You've got to close your eyes to see, he is here to set you free. And if you travel far from here, you will find him just as near. He is just a prayer away from you. And he is here to listen to you.

In the darkest of those lonely nights, he will shine like the brightest light. Jesus is the site for your sore eyes, and he is here to touch your life.

From the mountains to the prairies, across the oceans and the seas, we have gathered as one body. For we have come and we have seen.

Song Background

This song was written in 1997 for the pilgrimage to World Youth Day in Paris, France. "Site for Sore Eyes" highlights the need for us to understand and realize that Christ is always present to us. He is never far from us no matter where we are or where we go.

Related Scripture

Acts 17:26–28

Activities

Activities

Activity One
Leader Page

Site for Sore Eyes

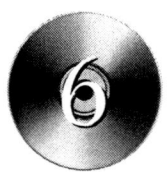

Written by Eric J. Sova

Activity Theme Prayer is a necessity within our faith lives. This activity helps to develop and challenge students to live a more prayerful life.

Preparation You will need the following items for this activity:
- Bibles for each student (or have them share)
- Writing utensil (1 per student)
- 1-inch wooden coin (1 per student – purchase at local craft store)
- Permanent marker (at least 1 per 4 students)
- Piece of scratch paper (1 per student)
- Candle
- Copy of Student Page (for each participant)

Opening Prayer Begin the session by having all of the students sit in one large circle around the lit candle. Have a student leader or an adult begin the session by reading the opening statement below. Then ask each student to offer a short prayer intention. This could be a short phrase or even just one word. (If your students have difficulty concentrating on the task, you might turn off all the lights and have everyone focus on the candle as a symbol of the light of Christ.) When finished, move on to the closing statement.

Opening Statement: Let us begin in the name of the Father, Son, and Holy Spirit. Heavenly Father, we thank you for this opportunity to gather together as young people to praise you and learn about you. As we gather, we leave our busy lives behind for a few minutes. In a short phrase or a simple word, we share with you the thoughts, concerns, and prayers that we bring with us today so you may lift these burdens from or hearts. We pray for….

Closing Statement: Father, we thank you for listening to us. Only you know all the prayers held within our hearts and spoken by our lips. Help us to understand your will so we may find peace within your love. Guide us in our daily lives and especially today as we open ourselves to you. We pray this in your name, our Lord, Jesus Christ. Amen.

Activities

Opening Activity Give each student a copy of the Student Page, a scratch sheet of paper, and a writing utensil. Ask the students to complete the Opening Activity on the Student Page. Make sure each student completes this activity on his or her own. When each student is finished, collect all of the scores and ask a couple adults to average each of the totals for you. Later in the activity, you will share the results of the poll.

Testimonial Ask a student leader or an adult to share a short testimonial about answered prayers in his or her life. Be sure to encourage them to talk about their daily prayer life and how that has benefited them. They may also want to share some of their favorite ways to pray, times to pray, and favorite prayers they recite.

Reflection Play the song "Site for Sore Eyes" and ask the students to follow along with the lyrics. After the song has played, share the results of your poll from the Opening Activity.

Activity Ask the students to gather into pairs and complete the Reflection questions on the Student Page. If time permits, you may formulate a comprehensive list of the types of prayer and suggested ways to make prayer a priority. This list would be a great handout during your next session that students could keep with them. You might also add some of the students' favorite prayers on the sheet so they can reference them when they need some help praying.

Challenge Give each student 1 wooden coin and a permanent marker. Ask each student to carefully print their first and last name on the coin. Make sure you can read it. Then collect all of the coins. Randomly hand out the coins to the group so no one has their original coin. Have the participants initial the back of the new coin. (Make sure the initials are small.) These are "prayer coins." As Christians, we are challenged to pray for one another. Therefore, challenge the students to carry the coin with them everywhere they go during the next week. Instruct them to pray for the person whose name appears on the coin any time they feel it in their pocket. Whenever they see each other at school, at work, or just hanging out with friends, they should swap coins so they get a new person to pray for. They should then initial the new coin. Eventually many of the coins will change hands several times. You might offer incentives for the person(s) whose initials show up on the most coins at the end of a week. Another idea is to create a prayer chain using this concept.

Activities

Activity One
Student Page

Site for Sore Eyes

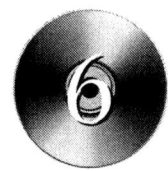

Written by Eric J. Sova

Opening Activity

On the scratch sheet of paper, list numbers 1 through 6. Do not write your name on the paper. Answer the following 6 questions; place your answers next to each of the corresponding numbers on your scratch paper. Be as honest as you possibly can. Remember…you are not putting your name on this.

1. On a scale of 1 to 10 (with 10 being the highest), how high of a priority is dedicated prayer in your personal life?

2. Yes or No. Do you truly believe that all prayers are answered in some way or another?

3. On average, how many minutes do you spend in dedicated prayer each week? (Please exclude any time you attend church or a youth function.)

4. How often do you pray a prayer of thanksgiving before each of your meals? 0–Never, 1–Rarely, 2–Occasionally, 3–More times than not, 4–All the time

5. Are you more likely to pray around your family or your friends?

6. What percentage of your friends would make fun of you for praying around them?

Fall on Your Knees · Site for Sore Eyes

Activities

Reflection Do not answer these questions until instructed to do so.

After listening to the song "Site for Sore Eyes" and sharing the results of the pool, answer the following 3 questions:

1. What surprised you about the results of the poll we did earlier? Why?
   _____
   _____

2. What did not surprise you? Why?
   _____
   _____

3. What does the song say about prayer?
   _____
   _____

Activity List 5 ways to pray.

1. _____
2. _____
3. _____
4. _____
5. _____

List 5 times when it is good to pray.

1. _____
2. _____
3. _____
4. _____
5. _____

Name your 2 favorite formal prayers and explain why they are your favorite.

1. _____
   _____
2. _____
   _____

Activities

Challenge   You have been given a wooden coin and a permanent marker. Print your first and last name on the coin. Make sure you can read it. In a minute all of the coins will be collected and then randomly redistributed so no one has their original coin. With small writing, initial the back of the new coin. These are "prayer coins." Carry them with you everywhere you go during the next week. Any time you feel this coin in your pocket, pray for the person whose name appears on it. Whenever you see another member of the group at school, at work, or just hanging out with your friends, swap coins so you get a new person to pray for. Immediately initial the new coin. Eventually many of the coins will change hands several times.

Activities

Activity Two
Leader Page

Site for Sore Eyes

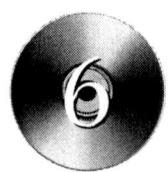

Written by Eric J. Sova

Activity Theme God is all around us, but many times we cannot see him. He calls us to find him, to look all around for him. This activity focuses on the need for young people to look all around and find God in all things.

Preparation You will need the following items for this activity:
- Bibles for each student (or have them share)
- Writing utensil (1 per student)
- Sheet of notebook paper (1 per student)
- Copies of a page from the book series Where's Waldo
- Large piece of banner paper
- Markers
- Copy of Student Page (for each participant)

Opening Prayer Ask a student leader or an adult to lead the group in a prayer that focuses on our need as Christians to find God in all that we do and in all people we come in contact with.

Opening Activity Gather the students in groups of four, and give them a copy of a page from the book series *Where's Waldo*. Give the students 5 to 10 minutes to find Waldo and as many other things as they can from a pre-set list. (Most of the books provide a complete list of items to find other than just Waldo.)

When the time is up, give each student a copy of the Student Page and ask them to answer the Opening Activity questions. (At the end of the session, you might project a copy of the puzzle on an overhead projector and have students point out all of the items from the list for the other students who might not have found them.)

Fall on Your Knees · Site for Sore Eyes

Activities

Testimonial   Ask a student leader or an adult share a short testimonial about a time in his or her life when he or she searched for God and found him. Be sure to ask them to include the frustrations they went through and then the joy they experienced when they found God in their situation.

Reflection   Ask the students to look up Acts 17:26–28 in their bibles. Have them answer the first Reflection question on the Student Page.

> Acts 17:26–28:
> He made from one the whole human race to dwell on the entire surface of the earth, and he fixed the ordered seasons and the boundaries of their regions so that people might seek God, even perhaps grope around for him and find him, though indeed he is not far from any one of us. For in him we live and move and have our being, as even some of your poets have said, "For we too are his offspring."

Then play the song "Site for Sore Eyes." Have the students finish the remaining Reflection questions. When finished, have them share their answers with a partner.

Challenge   Create a banner that reads, "We find God in…." On this banner, have the students write the answers they gave to the last Reflection question. Then challenge the students to find God in at least 1 additional aspect or thing in their lives for each day of the following week. Ask them to keep a list at the bottom of their Student Page. The next time you get together, collect all of the lists and add these to the banner. Hang the banner in an appropriate area of your gathering space for several weeks for everyone to see.

Activities

Activity Two
Student Page

Site for Sore Eyes

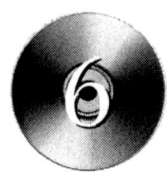

Written by Eric J. Sova

Opening Activity

1. What emotions do you feel when you cannot find an item on the list? Explain.

   _____
   _____

2. Did you give up on any items? If not, do you think it would be easy to do so? Why?

   _____
   _____

3. Patience is a personality trait that someone would need to be successful at this puzzle. List 5 more traits that would be beneficial.

   a. _____

   b. _____

   c. _____

   d. _____

   e. _____

Reflection

Look up Acts 17:26–28. Then answer the following question:

1. How does this scripture verse relate to the Opening Activity?

   _____
   _____

Fall on Your Knees · Site for Sore Eyes

Activities

Follow along to the lyrics of the song "Site for Sore Eyes." Then answer the following 4 questions:

1. What does this song have to say about finding God?

2. When is a time in your life that you have searched for God?

3. Why do you think God wants us to search for him?

4. List 5 aspects, people, or things in your life that you find God in.

   a.

   b.

   c.

   d.

   e.

Challenge Over the next week, look for God in your everyday life. Try to find God in at least 1 thing each day, and keep a list in the space provided below. The next time the group gets together, bring this sheet with your completed list so you can add your items to the "We found God in…" banner.

His Life

Written by Eric J. Sova

Lyrics

In the dead of night as I laid awake, I walked throughout my life. The thoughts slipped by of the times I've failed, and a tear fell from my eye. Cause if I could count the chances that were given in my life. I would go back to those chances and give them one more try. Here is my life. I'll give you all I have to give. Here is my life, my Lord.

Held by my fear and bound by concern, I start down this path. I've been here before with my heart all a mess. Look at the choices I've had. Cause if I could count the chances that were given in my life, I would go back to those chances and give them one more try.

The pain was real and the words were cruel, as He stumbled on His way. The weight of the world was upon His back, all of our sins He would pay. Cause if we would hear the message, of this man nailed to a cross, we would understand His reasons, to give us one more shot.

Here is His life. He gave us all He had to give. Here is His life, my friend.

Song Background

I wrote this song to parallel the human struggles we all go through with the struggle of Christ walking to be crucified. In the midst of our human struggle, we must give ourselves entirely to God just as Christ gave himself to us through his death on the cross. In this sacrifice, we are set free from our struggles if only we would use the chances we are given to change the way we live our lives.

Related Scripture

John 20:21–23
Luke 9:23–25

Activities

Activity One
Leader Page

His Life

Written by Eric J. Sova

Activity Theme

In life we are given a multitude of choices to make. As we go through our lives, we make many choices that we wish we could change. This activity helps us to look at ourselves and begin to realize the healing that can take place through giving our lives to Christ in the spirit of reconciliation.

Preparation

You will need the following items for this activity:
- Bibles for each student (or have them share)
- Writing utensil (1 per student)
- Sheet of notebook paper (1 per student)
- Candle
- Copy of Student Page (for each participant)
- Schedules for Sacrament of Reconciliation times at the church (business card size)

Opening Prayer

Ask a student leader or an adult to lead the group in a prayer that focuses on committing ourselves to walking in the footsteps of Christ. The prayer should talk about reconciliation, healing, and making positive choices.

Opening Activity

Give a copy of the Student Page to each of the students. Pair students up and ask them to answer the Opening Activity questions. Each of these questions asks students to explain their knowledge of the Sacrament of Reconciliation.

Presentation

Ask a student leader or an adult to give a short 5- to 10-minute presentation on the Sacrament of Reconciliation and the importance of going regularly. You will want to preview any presentation prior to your presenter sharing with your young people. The presenter should properly answer the questions that were asked in the Opening Activity. Use John 20:21–23 as a scriptural reference to get started.

Fall on Your Knees · His Life

Activities

Testimonial Ask a different student leader to share a short testimonial about how Reconciliation has brought peace and maybe even joy to his or her life. This should be a student leader (not an adult) because you would like other young people to see someone in their peer group who is excited about the Sacrament of Reconciliation.

Reflection Hand out a sheet of notebook paper to each student. Then have all the students gather together in a circle or half circle with the lit candle placed in the middle. Turn out all the lights and play the song "His Life." When the song is finished, ask the students to spread out in the room so they have their own personal space. (Don't forget to turn the lights back on.) Ask them to think over their last few weeks and months about all the times they wish they could go back and get "another chance" at a choice they had made. On the sheet of paper, ask them to write a journal letter to Christ that talks to him about these choices they would have changed. Then as they finish the letter, instruct them to, in their own words, "give their lives" once again to Christ.

Challenge Hand out the Reconciliation schedules and encourage the young people to pray about their journal letters and any other struggles they are currently going through. Then challenge them to pair up with a friend to go and receive the Sacrament of Reconciliation sometime during the next 2 weeks.

Activities

Activity One
Student Page

His Life

Written by Eric J. Sova

Opening Activity Pair up with a fellow student and answer the following 5 questions to the best of your ability.

1. In your own words, what is the Sacrament of Reconciliation?
   _____
   _____

2. Why is it important for a practicing Catholic to go the Sacrament of Reconciliation regularly?
   _____
   _____

3. How often does the Catholic Church recommend we should receive this Sacrament?
   _____
   _____

4. If we confess our sins directly to God in prayer, why do we still need to go to Reconciliation?
   _____
   _____

5. What other titles does the Sacrament of Reconciliation have?
   _____
   _____

Fall on Your Knees · His Life

Activities

Presentation In the space below, write down notes or phrases from the presentation that you would like to remember:

_____
_____
_____
_____
_____
_____

Reflection Do not complete this section until instructed to do so.

You have been given a sheet of notebook paper. Think over the last few weeks and months about all the times you wish you could go back and get "another chance" at a choice you had made. On the sheet of paper, write a journal letter to Christ that talks to him about these choices you made and would have liked to change. Before you finish the letter, make a commitment to God and yourself by stating in your own words that you "give your life" once again to Christ.

Challenge You have been given the schedule for the Sacrament of Reconciliation in your church. It is always easier to do things if you have someone who will go with you. Therefore, find a partner. Write your partner's name on the back of your schedule card along with a date and time when you will go to receive the Sacrament of Reconciliation in the next 2 weeks.

Activities

Activity Two
Leader Page

His Life

Written by Eric J. Sova

Activity Theme   There are times in our lives when we must carry our own crosses. Jesus calls us to drop what we are doing, pick up our cross, and follow him. This can be very difficult for some of us to do, but if we are going to give our lives to him, we must pick up our cross. This activity raises awareness of our need to bear our crosses for Christ.

Preparation   You will need the following items for this activity:
- Bibles for each student (or have them share)
- Writing utensil (1 per student)
- Small, wearable wooden crosses (1 per student – JustCatholic.com, approximately $3.00 each)
- Copy of Student Page (for each participant)

Opening Prayer   Ask a student leader or an adult to lead the group in a prayer that focuses on picking up our crosses to follow Jesus. The prayer should also address challenges young people face when turning away from the messages that mainstream society teaches and focusing on what Christ wants us to do.

Opening Activity   Give a copy of the Student Page to each of the students. Have the students find a partner. Then ask them to look up Luke 9:23–25 and answer the Opening Activity questions.

Luke 9:23-25:
> Then he said to all, "If anyone wishes to come after me, he must deny himself and take up his cross daily and follow me. For whoever wishes to save his life will lose it, but whoever loses his life for my sake will save it. What profit is there for one to gain the whole world yet lose or forfeit himself?"

Testimonial   Ask a student leader or an adult to give a short testimonial about a time in his or her life when he or she was called to pick up the cross and follow Christ. This could have been a change in career, a move, or a struggle with a medical condition. Be sure to include the rewards they received by giving themselves completely to Christ.

Reflection   Play the song "His Life." Ask the students to follow along with the lyrics of the song. After the song is finished, instruct the students to take 15 minutes and go into the church or other suitable area for prayer to think and pray about what crosses they have in their life that they must take up to give their lives more fully to Christ. It is important that they spend this time by themselves. When they are finished, have them answer the Reflection questions.

Challenge   Give each student a wearable wooden cross. Have the students inscribe on the cross the answer to the last Reflection question. Challenge the students to wear their crosses and pray that they may achieve whatever they have inscribed on their cross.

Activities

Activity Two
Student Page

His Life

Written by Eric J. Sova

Opening Activity

Look up Luke 9:23–25 and answer the following 4 questions:

1. What are the crosses that Christ is talking about in this scripture verse?

2. Why do you think Christ instructs us to pick up our cross?

3. What crosses do young people have in their daily lives?

4. Find one more scripture verse that talks about picking up your cross to follow Christ.

Reflection

Do not complete this section until instructed to do so.

Listen to the song "His Life" and follow along with the lyrics. You have been instructed to take some time and find a quiet place suitable for prayer. It is important that you find a place where you will not be disturbed by others, including your friends. This is your time with Christ. Think and pray about each of the following questions. In the space provided, write a short summary of your thoughts and prayers.

1. What is this song saying to you?

Fall on Your Knees · His Life

Activities

2. How does this song relate to your life?
   _____
   _____

3. What crosses do you have in your life that you need to pick up to follow Christ?
   _____
   _____

4. What is Christ calling you to do?
   _____
   _____

5. Of all of your crosses, which one is your greatest challenge?
   _____
   _____

Challenge You have been given a wooden cross. On that cross, write a short phrase that represents your answer to the last Reflection question. Wear this cross from now on as a reminder that you must pick up your cross and follow Christ. He calls us to give all of our life to him. Remember in your prayers over the next few weeks all of your crosses, especially the one you wear around your neck.

Wish

Written by Eric J. Sova

Activities

Lyrics

You will see me standing here and I will never walk away. I will hold you close to me. You're in my heart, can't you see? You're in my heart, can't you see?

Every evening at sunset I wish upon a star. Every evening I see you, I love the way you are. If only you'll love me and walk me through my life, every evening at sunset I'll wish upon your star.

Every morning I wake up and thank the Lord above. For this life he has given me, for the blessing of your love. I feel so thankful to have you standing by my side. Every evening at sunset I'll wish upon your star.

Every rainbow that brightens those rainy days of mine, holds a promise that love will last through every test of time. As the years go quickly by I pray to God tonight, may my wish come true as I wish upon your star.

Every evening at sunset I wish upon a star. Every evening I see you, I love the way you are. I know you'll love me and walk me through my life. Every evening at sunset I wish upon your star.

Song Background

Originally I wrote this song as a Christian love song. It has gradually taken on more meaning as a parallel to the love Christ has for each of us. His desire is for us to be with him, and in a way, he then "wishes on our stars." Jesus is always standing there and he will never walk away.

Related Scripture

1 Corinthians 13:4–7

Activities

Activity One
Leader Page

Wish

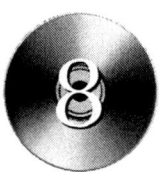

Written by Eric J. Sova

Activity Theme
Choose to love. This simple phrase is what each of us should remember whenever we are faced with a personal conflict with another person. When we choose to love, we imitate Christ's unconditional love for all of us. This activity teaches young people the importance of choosing to love.

Preparation
You will need the following items for this activity:
- Bibles for each student (or have them share)
- Writing utensil (1 per student)
- Video camera
- Copy of Student Page (for each participant)

Opening Prayer
Ask a student leader or an adult to lead the group in a prayer focused on unconditional love. They may use 1 Corinthians 13:4–7 as a starting point for the prayer.

Opening Activity
Give each student a copy of the Student Page and ask them to complete the Opening Activity questions in groups of four. These questions will allow students to spend some time in the bible looking for scriptures about love.

Testimonial
Ask a student or an adult leader to give a short testimonial about a time in his or her life when he or she was in a difficult situation and chose to love instead of the alternative. This could be a situation with a friend, family member, or significant other. Also include the reasons why they believe every situation in life should be approached with unconditional love.

Reflection
Play the song "Wish." Ask the students to follow along with the lyrics. When the song is finished, ask the students to complete the Reflection questions. When finished, have them share the answer to the last question with the large group. Be sure to ask them why they feel it relates to the song.

Challenge   If we choose to love, then we have love. Have the groups of four team up with another group so there are groups of eight. Give them 15 minutes to create a short, 15- to 30-second commercial around the theme "Got Love?" They should include at least some reference to one of the scripture readings they found in the Opening Activity. Use the video camera to record each of the group's commercials.

Activities

Activities

Activity One
Student Page

Wish

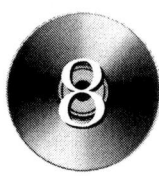

Written by Eric J. Sova

Opening Activity

In your groups, find as many scripture verses as you can that relate to the following aspects of unconditional love. After each scripture verse you find, write a short phrase that explains how this verse relates to love. Be sure to find at least 2 for each area.

Mary and Joseph's commitment to God:

1. _____
2. _____

God's greatest command:

1. _____
2. _____

Love one another:

1. _____
2. _____

Love your enemies:

1. _____
2. _____

God's love for His people:

1. _____
2. _____

Fall on Your Knees · Wish

Reflection Do not complete this section until instructed to do so.

After listening to the song "Wish," answer the following 3 questions:

1. What does the song say about love?

   _____
   _____

2. How does the song relate to God's love for us?

   _____
   _____

3. What scripture verse did you find in the Opening Activity that best relates to the song? Why?

   _____
   _____

Challenge You have been given 15 minutes to make a commercial based on the them "Got Love?" Use this outline to assist your efforts in creating your commercial. Be sure to use at least one of the scripture verses you found in the Opening Activity. Also, everyone in your group must play a role in your commercial.

Related scripture

_____
_____
_____

Setting:

_____
_____
_____

Roles:

_____
_____
_____

Order of events:

_____
_____
_____

Activities

Activities

Activity Two
Leader Page

Wish

Written by Eric J. Sova

Activity Theme One of the greatest desires a person seeks in life is true love. This activity will focus on defining the meaning of true love.

Preparation You will need the following items for this activity:
- Bibles for each student (or have them share)
- Writing utensil (1 per student)
- 3x5 index cards (1 per student)
- Copy of Student Page (for each participant)

Opening Prayer Ask a student leader or an adult to lead the group in a prayer that focuses on understanding the meaning of true love. Be sure to include aspects of Christ's love for those who follow him.

Opening Activity Give each student a copy of the Student Page and a writing utensil. Ask the students to complete the Opening Activity questions with a partner. Then have the students gather in groups of eight to discuss their answers with one another. Each pair should share with the other 3 pairs.

Presentation Ask a student leader or an adult to share for a few minutes on what the Church teaches us about true love and respect for human life. The focus on human life should focus on respecting one another and loving one another. What does the Church teach us about this kind of love? This should be no longer than 20 minutes in duration.

Reflection Play the song "Wish." Ask the students to think about the meaning of true love they discussed in the Opening Activity while they follow along with the lyrics. Once the song is finished, have them answer the Reflection questions on their own.

Challenge Give each student an index card. Ask the students to create a graphic symbol on the card that would remind them of the meaning of true love. This symbol should include all aspects of love for each other and love of Christ for us. Encourage the students to place the cards in a prominent place at home where they will see them often and be reminded that, as Christians, we are called to live a life based on true love.

Activities

Activities

Activity Two
Student Page

Wish

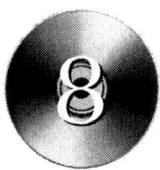

Written by Eric J. Sova

Opening Activity

Pair up with another student and then answer the following 4 questions:

1. When you hear the words "true love", what do you think this means?
   _____
   _____

2. How would you describe Christ's love for us?
   _____
   _____

3. How does Christ's love for us relate to what you think "true love" means?
   _____
   _____

4. Name a person in your life who you think lives a "true love" lifestyle. Why did you choose this person?
   _____
   _____

When finished, gather with 3 other pairs and share your answers to the above questions.

Presentation

Write 6 points from the presentation that you would like to remember in the future.

1. _____
2. _____
3. _____
4. _____

5. _____

6. _____

Reflection Listen to the song "Wish" and follow along with the lyrics. Think about the meaning of true love that you discussed in your groups. When the song is finished, spend a few minutes thinking about what this song is saying to you and then answer the following 2 questions:

1. What changes do you need to make in your life to live a "true love" lifestyle?

   _____
   _____
   _____

2. Do you think it is important to find friends who also live a "true love" lifestyle? Why or why not?

   _____
   _____
   _____

Challenge Do not complete this section until told to do so.

You have been given an index card. On this card, create a graphic symbol that would remind you of the meaning of true love. This symbol should include all aspects of love for each other and love of Christ for us. After you have completed your symbol, think of a prominent place at home where you can place your card. This way, every time you see it, you will be reminded that, as Christians, we are called to live a life based on true love.

Praise

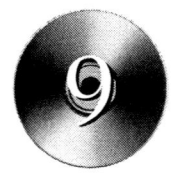

Written by Eric J. Sova

Lyrics *Praise God. Holy is the power of your name, Lord. Blessed be all glory to you.*

Raise your eyes to the heavens. Can you see the face of God? He has loved us. And he has held us. We must open our hearts to him.

Song Background This song was written to be a Praise and Worship piece. It has grown into a meditation and prayer song. There is a simple call within this song for people to focus on Christ.

Related Scripture Psalm 22:22–28
Philippians 4:6–7

Activities

Activities

Activity One
Leader Page

Praise

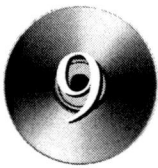

Written by Eric J. Sova

Activity Theme In every aspect of our lives, we need God. He is always there to answer our prayers. One thing we often forget to do is to thank him for the prayers he answers. This activity will focus on the need for us to be thankful to God.

Preparation You will need the following items for this activity:
- Bibles for each student (or have them share)
- Writing utensil (1 per student)
- Copy of Student Page (for each participant)

Opening Prayer Ask a student leader or an adult to lead the group in an opening prayer that focuses on giving thanks in our lives. The prayer should focus on praise and thanksgiving to God. Several common prayers of thanksgiving could be used.

Opening Activity Give each student a copy of the Student Page and a writing utensil. Ask the students to look up Philippians 4:6–7 and then answer the Opening Activity questions.

Philippians 4:6-7:
> Have no anxiety at all, but in everything, by prayer and petition, with thanksgiving, make your requests known to God. Then the peace of God that surpasses all understanding will guard your hearts and minds in Christ Jesus.

Testimonial Ask a student leader or an adult to share a short testimonial about a time in his or her life when he or she experienced an answered prayer that changed his or her life. Be sure to include how they gave thanks to God for answering their prayer.

Activities

Reflection Play the song "Praise." After the song is done playing, gather the students into groups of 6 to 8. Ask them to complete the Reflection activity. This activity allows students to form a greater understanding of why we give praise and thanksgiving to God. When they are finished with the activity, have each group appoint a spokesperson. Ask the spokesperson to present their statement of faith to the large group.

Challenge Over the next week, challenge the students to spend time prayerfully creating a list of requests from God. Then encourage the students to keep these lists in a safe place so they can live the call of Philippians 4:6–7 during their nightly prayers.

Activities

Activity One
Student Page

Praise

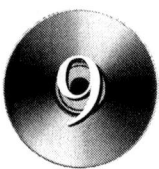

Written by Eric J. Sova

Opening Activity

Look up Philippians 4:6–7 in your bible and then answer the following 4 questions:

1. What does this scripture verse say to you?
   _____
   _____

2. Why is it important for us to always give thanks to God?
   _____
   _____

3. How often in your life do you forget to thank God for answered prayers?
   _____
   _____

4. What was the last answered prayer you received and did not say thanks for?
   _____
   _____

Reflection

Do not complete this section until instructed to do so.

Have one group member read off the following words one by one. After each word, write down the first word or phrase that comes to mind.

Praise: _____

God: _____

Prayer: _____

Thanksgiving: _____

Activities

Jesus: _____

Needs: _____

Glory: _____

Answers: _____

Name: _____

Holy: _____

Blessed: _____

Friends: _____

Share your answers with the rest of the group. Then answer the following 2 questions:

1. Are there any common themes in the group's answers? If Yes, what? If No, why not?
   _____
   _____
   _____

2. What do all these words have in common?
   _____
   _____
   _____

A statement of faith is a short paragraph that summarizes one's beliefs. An example would be the Apostles Creed.

As a group, create a statement of faith that would combine aspects from the song, the scripture verse from Philippians, and any common themes that were found in the group's answers above.

Challenge Over the next week, spend time prayerfully creating a list of requests for God. Keep these lists in a safe place so that, during your nightly prayers, you can live the call of Philippians 4:6–7 and pray to God for your needs, always giving thanks.

Activities

Activity Two
Leader Page

Praise

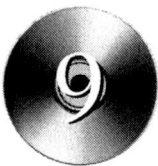

Written by Eric J. Sova

Activity Theme This activity will focus on Christ's true presence to each of us. Special emphasis is placed on creating and maintaining our relationship with him in our daily lives.

Preparation You will need the following items for this activity:
- Bibles for each student (or have them share)
- Writing utensil (1 per student)
- Small rock (1 per student)
- Copy of Student Page (for each participant)

Opening Prayer Ask a student leader or an adult to lead the group in an opening prayer that focuses on understanding that Christ is always there for us. It should address the reality that Jesus is a real person to us and that we ask for his presence in our daily lives.

Opening Activity Give each student a copy of the Student Page and a writing utensil. Ask the students to list 10 people they had face-to-face conversations with in the past couple of days. Then ask them to complete the Opening Activity questions.

Testimonial Ask a student leader or an adult to give a short testimonial about a time in his or her life when he or she knew Christ was truly present to him or her. Be sure to include the event, the feelings and, most of all, how they communicated with Christ. They might have several examples.

Reflection Gather the students into groups of four. Ask the students to complete the Reflection Activity. In this part of the activity, the students are asked to imagine Christ as a person they have a conversation with. They are asked to role-play these conversations. The final questions in the Reflection activity ask how we can find Christ truly present to us in our day-to-day lives. The primary answer we are looking for is that Christ is truly present to us when we pray, go to church, and celebrate the Eucharist. Christ is always there for us.

When finished, play the song "Praise." Ask the students to follow along with the lyrics and compare this song to how Christ is present to them.

Challenge   Give each student a small rock. Ask the students to examine their rock. With their rock hidden within their closed hand, have them describe their rock to a partner without letting the partner see it. This rock symbolizes the presence of Christ in our lives. Christ is always there in one form or another. He is the rock on which we build our faith. Challenge the students to carry their rock with them during the week as a reminder that Christ is always there for them; all they must do is open their hearts and minds in prayer.

Activities

Activities

Activity Two
Student Page

Praise

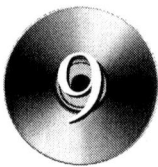

Written by Eric J. Sova

Opening Activity

List 10 people you had face-to-face conversations with in the past couple of days:

_____   _____
_____   _____
_____   _____
_____   _____
_____   _____

After you have completed your list, answer the following 2 questions.

1. Did the people on your list give you any advice or help with a problem?

   _____
   _____
   _____

2. In what ways were the people on your list truly present to you? Why?

   _____
   _____
   _____

Reflection

Gather into groups of four. What kinds of questions would you ask Jesus if you came face to face with him today? This part of the activity will ask you to do some role-playing. Choose one person who can play Jesus. Imagine yourself gathered with 2 of your friends and Jesus came up to you. Take the next 5 minutes and ask the person you selected as Jesus some of the questions you would want to ask Jesus if you came face to face with him. The person playing Jesus should attempt to answer the questions as if that person was really Jesus. After 5 minutes, switch roles.

Fall on Your Knees · Praise

Activities

When finished, answer the following 4 questions:

1. Do you think you can have a conversation with Jesus? Why or why not?

2. How difficult was it for the person playing Jesus to answer the questions that were posed?

3. How do we as Christians converse with Christ?

4. In these conversations with Christ, is there the opportunity for Christ to be truly present to us? How?

Now listen to the song "Praise" and answer the following question:

1. How does this song relate to how Christ is truly present to us?

Challenge   You have been given a small rock. Examine your rock carefully. Then with your rock hidden within your closed hand, describe your rock to a partner without letting your partner see it. This rock symbolizes the presence of Christ in our lives. Christ is always there in one form or another. He is the rock on which we build our faith. During the next week, carry your rock with you as a reminder that Christ is always there for us; all you must do is open your heart and mind in prayer and listen for Christ to be present to you.

Nails That Pierced

Written by Eric J. Sova

Lyrics *People gathered round that night as they raised Him high. Nailed to the wood of a cross, He was born to die. The priests were angry with His teaching, that there was only one truth. For He claimed he was a savior, this they would learn to realize.*

It's in the nails that pierced Him through His hands. It's in the nails that pierced the Son of man. As darkness fell upon the earth, we were saved from sin.

The thunder began to roll, as a cry went out. From the gash in His side, blood and water flowed out. He was a gateway for all people, to understand God's love. They had condemned Him to die but God would raise Him up.

Lord Jesus, save us.

Song Background I wrote this song to bring to life the passion of the Lord. The words create a powerful perspective of the sacrifice Christ gave to us just so we could be saved from our sins. We must always be thankful to God for giving us his son.

Related Scripture Psalm 22:13–18

Activities

Activity One
Leader Page

Nails That Pierced

Written by Eric J. Sova

Activity Theme The main purpose of this activity is to encourage the young people to have a better understanding and respect for the Passion of the Lord, as seen through the Stations of the Cross. They will place themselves in each of the stations.

Preparation You will need the following items for this activity:
- Bibles for each student (or have them share)
- Writing utensil (1 per student)
- Access to the Stations of the Cross (either in the church or create your own)
- Descriptions of each of the 14 Stations of the Cross
- Copy of Student Page (for each participant)

Opening Prayer Ask a student leader or an adult to lead the group in an opening prayer that focuses on guidance for the session—that the hearts and minds of the students gathered for this session will be touched by the story of Christ's walk to crucifixion.

Opening Activity Give each student a copy of the Student Page and a writing utensil. Play the song "Nails That Pierced" and then ask the students to answer the Opening Activity questions.

Testimonial Ask a student leader to give a short testimonial on how the Stations of the Cross have affected his or her life. They might even explain why it is important for us to experience the Stations.

Reflection Take the entire group to the location within your church or gathering space that has the Stations of the Cross. Instruct the students that as the group prayerfully walks from station to station, they should visualize themselves there in the crowd looking on as Christ struggles with each step. After a description of the Station is read, the students will draw an image of what they think the scene of that day looked like in the corresponding square on the Student Page. Once their picture is drawn, they should write a short prayer intention that relates to their life and that particular station. Do this for each of the 14 Stations of the Cross.

Stations of the Cross:
1. Jesus is condemned to die
2. Jesus carries his cross
3. Jesus falls for the first time
4. Jesus meets his mother
5. Simon of Cyrene helps Jesus carry the cross
6. Veronica wipes the face of Jesus
7. Jesus falls for the second time
8. Jesus consoles the weeping women
9. Jesus falls for the third time
10. Jesus is stripped of his clothes
11. Jesus is nailed to the cross
12. Jesus dies on the cross
13. Jesus is taken down from the cross
14. Jesus is laid in the tomb

Challenge

Ask each of the students to meditate on 2 of the stations they drew during their nightly prayers over the next week. Have them visualize what each station would have looked like. Then challenge each student to pray for the prayer intention they wrote. They may also include a prayer asking Christ to mold their lives after the example that he set by sacrificing his life for each of us.

Alternative Activities

- If your church is not already doing so, have the young people offer to host a Stations of the Cross Prayer Service for the entire church during the season of Lent.

- Find a local retreat site, monastery, mission, etc., that has an outdoor Stations of the Cross and take a pilgrimage to that location.

Activities

Activity One
Student Page

Nails That Pierced

Written by Eric J. Sova

Opening Activity

Answer the following 2 questions about the song "Nails That Pierced."

1. What message do you hear in this song (not including the fact that Christ died to save us)?

   _____
   _____

2. How does this song make you feel about the people who watched Christ be sent to his crucifixion?

   _____
   _____

Reflection

Do not complete this section until instructed to do so.

Below you will see 14 boxes. As you hear the description of each Station of the Cross, draw a picture in the corresponding box of what you would see as a young person if you were actually there watching Jesus. Be as detailed as you can in the time provided for each station. When you are finished with your drawing, write a short prayer intention that relates to your life and the current Station of the Cross.

Activities

1. Jesus is condemned to die

2. Jesus carries his cross

Fall on Your Knees · Nails That Pierced

Activities

3. Jesus falls for the first time

4. Jesus meets his mother

5. Simon of Cyrene helps Jesus carry the cross

6. Veronica wipes the face of Jesus

Fall on Your Knees • Nails That Pierced

Activities

7. Jesus falls for the second time

8. Jesus consoles the weeping women

Fall on Your Knees · Nails That Pierced

Activities

9. Jesus falls for the third time

10. Jesus is stripped of his clothes

Fall on Your Knees · Nails That Pierced

Activities

11. Jesus is nailed to the cross

12. Jesus dies on the cross

Fall on Your Knees · Nails That Pierced

Activities

13. Jesus is taken down from the cross

14. Jesus is laid in the tomb

Fall on Your Knees · Nails That Pierced

Activities

Challenge During your nightly prayers over the next week, take a few minutes to meditate on 2 of the stations you drew. Visualize the scene with the crowd and a tired, beaten Jesus struggling to walk to his death. After you have prayed about and visualized those particular stations, take a few more minutes to pray for the prayer intentions you wrote for each of those 2 stations.

Activities

Activity Two
Leader Page

Nails That Pierced

Written by Eric J. Sova

Activity Theme

The nails that were hammered into the wrists and feet of Christ are representative of the sins that each of us bears. Christ took those sins away with his death on the cross. This activity focuses on the need for us as Christians to turn away from our sins.

Preparation

You will need the following items for this activity:
- Bibles for each student (or have them share)
- Writing utensil (1 per student)
- Strips of paper, 1 by 8 inches (at least 5 per student)
- Scotch tape
- Large cross
- Small finishing nails, approximately 2 inches long (1 per student)
- Copy of Student Page (for each participant)

Set up the large cross in the front of the room.

Opening Prayer

Ask a student leader or an adult to lead the group in an opening prayer that focuses on the need for us as Christians to turn away from our sins. Use the Our Father prayer as a starting point.

Opening Activity

Give each student a copy of the Student Page and a writing utensil. Ask the students to list at least 10 sins they think young people routinely commit. These do not have to be sins they have committed. When they are finished with their list, have them choose the top 5 and write each one on a strip of paper. Take each of the pieces of paper and start to form a paper chain. Continue adding all of the strips until every chain is connected. Once this is finished, drape the chain over the large cross. Try to keep all of the chain on the cross.

Fall on Your Knees · Nails That Pierced

Activities

Testimonial   Ask a student leader or an adult to give a short testimonial that focuses on a time in his or her life when he or she experienced the joy of forgiveness. They might relate it to the forgiveness that Christ gives to each one of us through his death and resurrection.

Reflection   Read the following to the students:

> This chain represents the sins that keep us from Christ's love. How many of these links of the chain contain sins you have committed? In Christ's crucifixion, we were saved from these chains. But how many of us continue to build new chains in our daily lives? Take a moment to listen to the words of the song "Nails That Pierced." Think and pray about the chains on this cross that you have built.

Play the song "Nails That Pierced." Ask the students to follow along with the lyrics. When the song is finished, ask the students to complete the Reflection questions on the Student Page.

Challenge   Give each student 1 of the finishing nails. Challenge the students to carry the nail around with them over the next several weeks. Whenever they feel the nail or poke themselves with it, let them be reminded of the nails that were driven through the wrists and feet of Christ so our chains of sin would be broken.

Activities

Activity Two
Student Page

Nails That Pierced

Written by Eric J. Sova

Opening Activity

List at least 10 sins you think young people routinely commit:

1. _____
2. _____
3. _____
4. _____
5. _____
6. _____
7. _____
8. _____
9. _____
10. _____

Choose the 5 you think are the most common and place a star next to them.

Reflection

Do not complete this section until instructed to do so.

After listening to the song "Nails That Pierced," answer the following 4 questions:

Activities

1. What was your initial reaction once all the chains were piled onto the cross?

   _____
   _____
   _____

2. What does the song say about the saving power of Christ?

   _____
   _____
   _____

3. Why do you think it is so easy for us to create more chains?

   _____
   _____
   _____

4. What can you do in your life to break the chains you create?

   _____
   _____
   _____

Challenge You have been given a nail. Carry this nail with you during the next several weeks. If you reach into your pocket and feel the nail or poke yourself, let it remind you of the nails that were driven into the wrists and feet of Christ so you could be set free from your chains of sin. During your nightly prayers, remember the times you have been bound by these chains, and pray that Christ may help you avoid them in the future.

This Is Your Choice

Activities

Written by Eric J. Sova

Lyrics

We had talked about it that one day, then we went our separate ways. I never knew what you planned to do, but I said all I could say. Well the time would come when you'd make your choice. When you're tempted by wrong, you can hold on strong.

He was calling out your name. Telling you don't or you'll never be the same. This is your choice you have to make. When you're tempted by wrong, then you'll know…Jesus is the way.

When you stand here today and you make your choice. You've changed your life forever by committing to his challenge. When we send you from here, you become the voice. You can help them to live by the faith that you give.

You can change the life of a friend with the words that Jesus said. Lead them on to a better life. It's a choice you make, to walk in the light.

Song Background

This song was originally written for a "True Love Waits" campaign. Before it was recorded on the Fall project, most of the lyrics where modified to include all choices someone could make—not just the choice to live a chaste lifestyle. Most negative choices are easy to make, whereas the right choices can sometimes be tough to make. We can take comfort in knowing that if we live our lives like Christ, then we will make the right choices. When it gets difficult, we can always hold on strong to Christ.

Related Scripture

John 8:1–11

Activities

Activity One
Leader Page

This Is Your Choice

Written by Eric J. Sova

Activity Theme The mainstream media constantly bombards us to live in the moment regardless of what we believe or what our morals may be. We have 2 choices in life: to be true to the way of Jesus or to reject it. This activity will help young people examine their own lives to see if they are living as Jesus would want them to live.

Preparation You will need the following items for this activity:
- Bibles for each student (or have them share)
- Writing utensil (1 per student)
- Large adhesive labels, approximately 4 by 11 inches (1 per pair of students)
- Markers
- Large sheet of banner paper
- Copy of Student Page (for each participant)

Opening Prayer Ask a student leader or an adult to lead the group in an opening prayer that focuses on the choices young people must make every day. The prayer should touch on all aspects of a student's life—school, work, friends, family, and other activities.

Opening Activity Give each student a copy of the Student Page and a writing utensil. Ask the students to complete the Opening Activity questions.

Testimonial Ask a student leader or an adult to share a short testimonial about a time in his or her life when he or she was challenged to follow Christ even though it was not the popular thing to do at the time. Be sure to include the challenges that were faced and how they were overcome.

Reflection Play the song "This Is Your Choice." Ask the students to follow along with the lyrics. When the song is finished, pair up the students and give each pair a large adhesive label. Ask the students to answer the Reflection questions and then create a unique slogan that focuses on the idea of living a Christ-like life. An example of this kind of slogan would be the "WWJD" or "What Would Jesus Do?" that was so popular. Encourage the students to make their slogan different.

Following are some guidelines for the slogans:

- Make it easy to remember.
- Make it unique.
- Include a theme from the song "This Is Your Choice."

When students are done creating their slogans, have them randomly stick the labels on the banner paper. If time permits, ask each pair to explain their slogan to the large group.

Challenge Ask the students to choose 3 of the slogans they can relate to from the banner and to write them on their Student Page. Encourage the students to find a way to incorporate these slogans into their daily lives so they will remember them when a time comes to make a choice to follow Christ or follow the crowd.

Activities

Activity One
Student Page

This Is Your Choice

Written by Eric J. Sova

Opening Activity

Everything in life is choice. There are good choices and there are bad choices. Think about your last week, and list 5 good and 5 bad choices you made.

Good

1. _____
2. _____
3. _____
4. _____
5. _____

Bad

1. _____
2. _____
3. _____
4. _____
5. _____

Then answer the following 3 questions:

1. Why is it sometimes hard to make the right choice?

   _____
   _____
   _____

2. How large of an impact do your friends have on the moral choices you make? Why?

_____
_____

3. Name one friend you think is a great role model for you? Why?

_____
_____

Reflection Do not complete this section until instructed to do so.

After listening to the song "This Is Your Choice," answer the following 2 questions:

1. What does the song tell you about the choices you must make in your life?

_____
_____

2. What changes in your life must you make to become a positive influence on your friends?

_____
_____

You have been given a large adhesive label. On this label, create a slogan that focuses on how you should live a Christ-like life. Think about the popular "WWJD" or "What Would Jesus Do?" slogan. This is the type of slogan you want to create, but make yours should be unique. It should also include one of the themes from the song "This Is Your Choice." Most importantly, you want it to be something that is easy to remember. Use the space below to develop some ideas. Once you have decided on the perfect slogan, use markers to create your label.

_____
_____
_____
_____
_____
_____
_____

Fall on Your Knees · This Is Your Choice

Activities

Challenge Write down 3 slogans you can relate to. Find a way to incorporate these slogans into your daily life so you will remember them when the time comes to make a difficult choice.

1. _____
2. _____
3. _____

Activities

Activity Two
Leader Page

This Is Your Choice

Written by Eric J. Sova

Activity Theme

One of the ways we commit ourselves to Christ is by living a life of stewardship. Stewardship incorporates 3 things: our time, our talent, and our treasure. This activity provides an opportunity for students to discover where they may be called to share their talents in the church community.

Preparation

You will need the following items for this activity:
- Bibles for each student (or have them share)
- Writing utensil (1 per student)
- Several speakers from the different church ministries
- Sign-up sheets (for different speakers)
- Copy of Student Page (for each participant)

Opening Prayer

Ask a student leader or an adult to lead the group in an opening prayer that focuses on the idea of stewardship in one's life. Be sure to include all 3 aspects of stewardship: time, talent, and treasure.

Opening Activity

Give each student a copy of the Student Page and a writing utensil. Have the students get into pairs and ask them to look up the Parable of the Talents, Matthew 25:14–30. After they have reviewed this parable, ask them to complete the Opening Activity questions. You may have to assist the students with the definitions of stewardship.

Matthew 25:14–30:
> It will be as when a man who was going on a journey called in his servants and entrusted his possessions to them. To one he gave five talents; to another, two; to a third, one—to each according to his ability. Then he went away. Immediately the one who received five talents went and traded with them and made another five. Likewise, the one who received two made another two. But the man who received one went off and dug a hole in the ground and buried his master's money.

After a long time the master of those servants came back and settled accounts with them. The one who had received five talents came forward bringing the additional five. He said, "Master, you gave me five talents. See, I have made five more."

His master said to him, "Well done, my good and faithful servant. Since you were faithful in small matters, I will give you great responsibilities. Come, share your master's joy."

Then the one who had received two talents also came forward and said, "Master, you gave me two talents. See, I have made two more."

His master said to him, "Well done, my good and faithful servant. Since you were faithful in small matters, I will give you great responsibilities. Come, share your master's joy."

Then the one who had received the one talent came forward and said, "Master, I knew you were a demanding person, harvesting where you did not plant and gathering where you did not scatter; so out of fear I went off and buried your talent in the ground. Here it is back."

His master said to him in reply, "You wicked, lazy servant! So you knew that I harvest where I did not plant and gather where I did not scatter? Should you not then have put my money in the bank so that I could have got it back with interest on my return? Now then! Take the talent from him and give it to the one with ten. For to everyone who has, more will be given and he will grow rich; but from the one who has not, even what he has will be taken away. And throw this useless servant into the darkness outside, where there will be wailing and grinding of teeth."

STEWARDSHIP OF TIME – volunteering your time in service to one another (e.g., helping out at soup kitchen, Meals on Wheels, assisting the elderly)

STEWARDSHIP OF TALENT – using the gifts God gave you in service to one another (e.g., singing, lectoring, decorating)

Activities

STEWARDSHIP OF TREASURE – giving a percentage of your financial wealth to the church, also known as *tithing*

Presentation   Contact several people from the different church ministries and ask them to come and give a short, 1- to 3-minute presentation on what their ministry is about and how students can get involved. Ask the students to take notes of what ministries they would like to be a part of; then at the end of all of the presentations, allow students to sign up for the ministry or ministries of their choice.

Testimonial   Ask a student leader who is involved in one or more ministries in the church to share a short testimonial about how volunteering in a ministry has changed his or her life. They might also want to share how their stewardship has impacted their daily life.

Reflection   Play the song "This Is Your Choice." Ask the students to answer the Reflection questions on the Student Page as they relate to the song and the Testimonial.

Challenge   Challenge each student to become trained in at least 1 ministry during the next several months. One method of doing this is to have every student make a commitment to at least 1 ministry and sign his or her name to a commitment sheet. You can then follow up with those students in a few weeks to see if they have received training or if they have any questions.

Activity Two
Student Page

This Is Your Choice

Written by Eric J. Sova

Opening Activity

Each of us is called to live a life of stewardship. This means we are called to give of our time, talent, and treasure in service to one another. Look up the Parable of the Talents, Matthew 25:14–30, and then answer the following 4 questions with your partner:

1. What message does Christ give with this parable?

2. How does this apply to a young person's life?

3. In your own words, give definitions for the 3 areas of stewardship: time, talent, and treasure.

4. Why are we called to live as good stewards?

Presentation

Use the space below to take any notes or jot down any questions about the ministries that are being presented to you.

Reflection Listen to the song "This Is Your Choice." Then answer the following 2 questions:

1. What does this song have to say about stewardship?

2. What similarities can you see in the meaning of this song and the call that was answered by the person giving the testimonial?

Challenge Prayerfully consider signing up for at least 1 of the ministries presented today. This is just one way that you can live a life of stewardship. If you are uncertain that you would like to do a certain ministry by yourself, encourage a friend to sign up with you. One thing to remember is that once you have committed yourself, you cannot "hide" from your ministry. On the contrary, you should commit yourself to being a good steward and staying active.

Part 2
The Prayer Services

Prayer Service

Remember Me

Written by Eric J. Sova and Joseph Mills

Preparation You will need the following items for this prayer service:
- 2 candles
- Cross or crucifix
- Meditation music
- Journal book (or something similar for prayer intentions)

Environment Place the cross at the front of the room with the candles on either side. Place the journal book on a stand in front of the cross. If possible, dim the room's lights so there is just enough light to read. You want to create an environment that will assist your students to devote themselves to prayer. Have the meditation music playing as students gather for the prayer service. If possible, set up the chairs into 2 groups that face each other.

Gathering Invite students to take a few moments to reflect upon the past couple of days—what has happened to them at school, at home, and in their activities. Give them a moment to quiet themselves and bring themselves into the presence of Christ.

Opening Prayer (Read in the front of the room, slowly and prayerfully.)
(stand)

Leader: We begin in the name of the Father and of the Son and of the Holy Spirit. Amen.

My dear friends, Christ calls us to realize that he is always with us. No matter what is happening in our lives or how far we stray from him, he is always with us. We open our hearts to feel what we need to feel. We open our ears to hear what we need to hear. We open our minds to learn what we need to learn.

Prayer Services

We come together today to share our lives with each other. We come together to ask Christ to send the Holy Spirit to lead us in our faith journey. We come together as one united by Christ's presence.

Heavenly Father, we come before you today as your humble servants. Some of us come before you with questions, others with a heavy heart, and still others with a desire to welcome you into our hearts more fully. Bless our time together. May we feel your presence, Lord. We ask this in your name, our Lord Jesus Christ.

All: Amen

(sit)

Readings

Reader: A reading from the second letter of Paul to the Corinthians. (2 Corinthians 1:3–10)

Blessed be the God and Father of our Lord Jesus Christ, the Father of compassion and God of all encouragement, who encourages us in our every affliction, so that we may be able to encourage those who are in any affliction with the encouragement with which we ourselves are encouraged by God. For as Christ's sufferings overflow to us, so through Christ does our encouragement also overflow. If we are afflicted, it is for your encouragement and salvation; if we are encouraged, it is for your encouragement, which enables you to endure the same sufferings that we suffer. Our hope for you is firm, for we know that as you share in the sufferings, you also share in the encouragement.

We do not want you to be unaware, brothers, of the affliction that came to us in the province of Asia; we were utterly weighed down beyond our strength, so that we despaired even of life. Indeed, we had accepted within ourselves the sentence of death, that we might trust not in ourselves but in God who raises the dead. He rescued us from such great danger of death, and he will continue to rescue us; in him we have put our hope that he will also rescue us again.

The word of the Lord.

All: Thanks be to God.

(stand)

Reader 2: A reading from the Gospel according to John. (John 15:1–11)

All: Glory to you, O Lord.

Reader 2: I am the true vine, and my Father is the vine grower. He takes away every branch in me that does not bear fruit, and everyone that does he prunes so that it bears more fruit. You are already pruned because of the word that I spoke to you. Remain in me, as I remain in you. Just as a branch cannot bear fruit on its own unless it remains on the vine, so neither can you unless you remain in me. I am the vine, you are the branches. Whoever remains in me and I in him will bear much fruit, because without me you can do nothing. Anyone who does not remain in me will be thrown out like a branch and wither; people will gather them and throw them into a fire and they will be burned. If you remain in me and my words remain in you, ask for whatever you want and it will be done for you. By this is my Father glorified, that you bear much fruit and become my disciples. As the Father loves me, so I also love you. Remain in my love. If you keep my commandments, you will remain in my love, just as I have kept my Father's commandments and remain in his love. "I have told you this so that my joy may be in you and your joy may be complete.

The Gospel of the Lord.

All: Praise to you, Lord Jesus Christ.

(sit)

Reflection

(Following the readings, a short period of sharing should be done that talks about the readings and a related personal story.)

Leader: Jesus has promised us that he will never leave us, especially in our time of need. In a moment, I would like to invite you to come forward and sign our book of intentions. Feel free to write a short prayer intention for something that has been weighing on your heart. Jesus once said, "Where two or more of you are gathered, I am there." Today we ask for his presence.

(Play the song "Remember Me" as students sign book of prayer intentions. When everyone is finished signing the book of intentions, the leader will retrieve the book and hold it while the closing prayer is said.)

Leader: Christ taught us how to pray; therefore, we join together as one body as we pray.

All: *(recite the Lord's Prayer)*

Closing Prayer

Leader: Father, thank you for the many blessings you have poured upon us. We thank you for listening to our prayers and leading us in the direction we should go. We place before you our concerns, our wants, our sufferings. We ask that you continue to remember us in our good times and in our darkest hour. May you hear the prayers written within our book of intentions and answer them according to your will. Heavenly Father, please bless our week ahead. And may we be true stewards of our gifts.

We thank you and offer this in your name, Lord Jesus Christ.

All: Amen.

Leader: Let us go forth in the name of the Father and of the Son and of the Holy Spirit.

All: Amen.

(An appropriate closing song could be chosen, or replay "Remember Me.")

Prayer Service

Reflect the Light

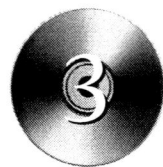

Written by Eric J. Sova and Joseph Mills

Preparation — You will need the following items for this prayer service:
- Large votive candles
- Large wooden cross
- Lit Easter candle
- Candles with drip cups (1 per student)

Environment — Place the large cross in the front of the room with the votive candles on one side and the lit Easter candle on the other.

Gathering — Invite students to take a few moments to reflect upon the past couple of days—what has happened to them at school, at home, and in their activities. Give them a moment to quiet themselves and bring themselves into the presence of Christ.

Opening Prayer — (Read in the front of the room, slowly and prayerfully.)
(stand)

Leader: We begin in the name of the Father and of the Son and of the Holy Spirit. Amen.

All gracious and loving God, we thank you for the gifts you give to us. We also thank you for the gift of each other. We ask for the courage to answer your call for us. We ask for strength to endure the hardships that may come with that call. And we ask for wisdom as you guide us on this journey. We ask this in your name, our Lord, Jesus Christ.

All: Amen.

(sit)

Readings

Reader: A reading from the Gospel according to Matthew.
(Matthew 5:13–16)

All: Glory to you, O Lord.

Reader: You are the salt of the earth. But if salt loses its taste, with what can it be seasoned? It is no longer good for anything but to be thrown out and trampled underfoot. You are the light of the world. A city set on a mountain cannot be hidden. Nor do they light a lamp and then put it under a bushel basket; it is set on a lamp stand, where it gives light to all in the house. Just so, your light must shine before others, that they may see your good deeds and glorify your heavenly Father.

The Gospel of the Lord.

All: Praise to you, Lord Jesus Christ.

Reflection

(Leader should give a short sharing about the importance of being a light for the world.)

Leader: We are called to be holy, and through our holiness we become lights for the world. In our baptism we were given the light of Christ so it would burn within our hearts. I now call you to come forward and once again receive the light of Christ.

(Play the song "Reflect the Light" as each student comes forward and receives a candle. After the students are given a candle, have them light it from the Easter candle and then return to their seats. Once the song is finished, continue with the closing prayer.)

Closing Prayer

Leader: We have once again received the light of Christ. We are called to spread this light in all that we do. Christ calls us every day to be lights for the world, and by accepting these candles we pledge our lives to spreading the light. It shall not be extinguished by us but rather spread like wildfire.

Lord Jesus, we ask you to send us your Spirit to be our helping hand as we are sent out to witness to all those we come in contact with. May we touch those lives and lead them to your love. Grant this, Christ, the Lord.

All: Amen.

Leader: Let us go forth in the name of the Father and of the Son and of the Holy Spirit.

All: Amen.

Prayer Service

Fall (On Your Knees)

Written by Eric J. Sova and Joseph Mills

Preparation You will need the following items for this prayer service:
- Large wooden cross
- Large votive candles
- Access to Blessed Sacrament for Adoration

Environment Set up the cross in the front of the room with the votive candles set to either side of the cross. If you do not have access to an Adoration Chapel, you will need to create a space in a separate room for Eucharistic Adoration. You will need a monstrance and several candles. Do not put out the Blessed Sacrament if there is no one in the room. Instead, wait until you begin Adoration or get someone to be present with the Blessed Sacrament when the rest of the group can be there. If you are not familiar with how Eucharistic Adoration is supposed to be done, please contact your pastor at the parish for assistance. It is extremely important that this is done properly and reverently.

Gathering Gather in the room in which you set up the large cross. Invite students to take a few moments to reflect upon the past couple of days—what has happened to them at school, at home, and in their activities. Give them a moment to quiet themselves and bring themselves into the presence of Christ.

Opening Prayer (Read in the front of the room, slowly and prayerfully.)
(stand)

Leader: We begin in the name of the Father and of the Son and of the Holy Spirit. Amen.

Lord Jesus, we thank you for the gift of life. We thank you for the opportunity to gather as one in your name and celebrate our faith. We ask that you make yourself present to us today during our time of prayer. We ask this in your name, our Lord, Jesus Christ.

All: Amen.

(sit)

Readings

Reader: A reading from the Gospel according to John. (John 6:45–58)

All: Glory to you, O Lord.

Reader: It is written in the prophets: "They shall all be taught by God. Everyone who listens to my Father and learns from him comes to me. Not that anyone has seen the Father except the one who is from God; he has seen the Father. Amen, amen, I say to you, whoever believes has eternal life. I am the bread of life. Your ancestors ate the manna in the desert, but they died; this is the bread that comes down from heaven so that one may eat it and not die. I am the living bread that came down from heaven; whoever eats this bread will live forever; and the bread that I will give is my flesh for the life of the world."

The Jews quarreled among themselves, saying, "How can this man give us [his] flesh to eat?" Jesus said to them, "Amen, amen, I say to you, unless you eat the flesh of the Son of Man and drink his blood, you do not have life within you. Whoever eats my flesh and drinks my blood has eternal life, and I will raise him on the last day. For my flesh is true food, and my blood is true drink. Whoever eats my flesh and drinks my blood remains in me and I in him. Just as the living Father sent me and I have life because of the Father, so also the one who feeds on me will have life because of me. This is the bread that came down from heaven. Unlike your ancestors who ate and still died, whoever eats this bread will live forever."

The Gospel of the Lord.

All: Praise to you, Lord Jesus Christ.

Reflection

Leader: In a few moments we will be spending some personal time before the Blessed Sacrament.

This is an opportunity to spend some time directly with Christ. We must realize that Christ is a real person who we can go to for assistance at any time. Just like we go to a best friend for help or advice, we, too, go to Christ for answers to life's challenges. We also go to Christ to thank him for the blessings that he bestows upon our lives. One of the easiest ways to place ourselves in the presence of Christ is through Eucharistic Adoration. This is a time of prayer, conversation, and especially listening for our Lord Jesus to speak to your heart. Adoration allows us one-on-one time with Jesus. Block out all other distractions you have in your life and concentrate on Christ's true presence to you during this time.

As we prepare to spend this very personal time with Jesus, let us take a moment and reflect upon our own lives. Listen to the words from the song "Fall (On Your Knees)." Do you fall on your knees when the world knocks you down, or do you run from your God whom you fear? Do you lose all your faith when your friends cut it down? Or do you know that he is near? Do you know that Christ is here?

(Play the song "Fall (On Your Knees).")

Leader: When you are ready, please feel free to move to the Adoration Chapel. Please remember that this is a time of prayer. We can gather back together in approximately 30 minutes.

(Move to the Adoration Chapel. Once everyone has gathered back into the original room, continue with the closing prayer. Split the group into boys and girls—or any other equal division.)

Closing Prayer

Leader: Let us close in prayer. Father, thank you for this personal time that we have spent with you. May we never take you for granted. Bless our week ahead and help us to walk in your footsteps.

Girls: Watch over us and protect us, Lord .

Boys: We humbly present you this prayer.

Girls: Call us to be your servants, Lord.

Boys: We are here to answer the call.

Girls: May the Lord always bless us.

Boys: Strengthen and mold us in your presence.

Leader: We ask this in the name of Christ, our Lord and Savior.

All: Amen.

Leader: Let us go forth in the name of the Father and of the Son and of the Holy Spirit.

All: Amen.

Prayer Service
Stand Up

Preparation You will need the following items for this prayer service:
- Large wooden cross
- Statue of the Blessed Virgin Mary
- Roses or carnations (1 per participant)
- Printed index cards with the words, "I say YES to God's call in my life."
- Candles (optional)

Environment Set up the large wooden cross and the statue of the Blessed Virgin Mary in the front of the room. Place the roses or carnations at the foot of Mary or in a vase directly next to the statue. If candles are desired, place them next to the statue as well. Place the index cards in a stack close to the foot of Mary and easily accessible by all participants.

Gathering Invite students to take a few moments to reflect upon the past couple of days—what has happened to them at school, at home, and in their activities. Give them a moment to quiet themselves and bring themselves into the presence of Christ.

Opening Prayer (Read in the front of the room, slowly and prayerfully.)
(stand)

Leader: We begin in the name of the Father and of the Son and of the Holy Spirit. Amen.

Holy Father, we thank you for the gift of life. We thank you for always calling us to a life of holiness. We ask you to continue to teach us, to guide us, and to walk with us in our daily journey of faith. Help us to follow the example set by your mother, the Blessed Virgin Mary, in her life of holiness and service. We ask this in your name, our Lord, Jesus Christ.

All: Amen.

Leader: We are called to be holy. (pause)
We are called to be servants. (pause)

> We are called to love one another. *(pause)*
> We are called to follow the Lord. *(pause)*
> We are called to say, "Yes." *(pause)*
> We are called to follow the example of Mary. *(pause)*

Leader: Hail Mary, full of grace, the Lord is with you. Blessed are you among women and blessed is the fruit of your womb. Holy Mary, Mother of God, pray for us sinners now and at the hour of our death.

(sit)

Readings

Reader: A reading from the Gospel according to Luke.
(Luke 1:26–38)

All: Glory to you, O Lord.

Reader: In the sixth month, the angel Gabriel was sent from God to a town of Galilee called Nazareth, to a virgin betrothed to a man named Joseph, of the house of David, and the virgin's name was Mary. And coming to her, he said, "Hail, favored one! The Lord is with you." But she was greatly troubled at what was said and pondered what sort of greeting this might be. Then the angel said to her, "Do not be afraid, Mary, for you have found favor with God. Behold, you will conceive in your womb and bear a son, and you shall name him Jesus. He will be great and will be called Son of the Most High, and the Lord God will give him the throne of David his father, and he will rule over the house of Jacob forever, and of his kingdom there will be no end." But Mary said to the angel, "How can this be, since I have no relations with a man?" And the angel said to her in reply, "The Holy Spirit will come upon you, and the power of the Most High will overshadow you. Therefore, the child to be born will be called holy, the son of God. And behold, Elizabeth, your relative, has also conceived a son in her old age, and this is the sixth month for her who was called barren; for nothing will be impossible for God." Mary said, "Behold, I am the handmaid of the Lord. May it be done to me according to your word." Then the angel departed from her.

The Gospel of the Lord.

All: Praise to you, Lord Jesus Christ.

(sit)

Leader: Mary trusted in her faith and said "Yes" to God. We, too, must trust in our faith and say "Yes" to the Lord in our daily lives. We are truly called to be disciples of Christ. He wants us to walk in his footsteps and lead others to him. We must stand up and answer this call. The song "Stand Up" challenges us to stand up for our faith. It also reminds us that we cannot be afraid to fall. When we answer the call of Jesus, just as Mary did, our hopes and our dreams will be realized.

(Play the song "Stand Up.")

Reflection

Leader: Take a moment to reflect upon your own life. How can you answer God's call and stand up for your faith? *(pause)*

Did you know you do not need to go at this alone? *(pause)*
Did you know that there is someone there to pray for you in your journey? *(pause)*
Did you know that all you needed to do was ask for help? *(pause)*

Mary is always there to intercede for you. All you have to do is ask her to pray for you. Today we turn to her and ask her to do just that. We ask her to pray for us.

(Invite the group to join in saying a rosary. If your group is unfamiliar with how to say a rosary, take a few moments to explain how and why we say rosaries. Use the Joyful Mysteries.)

Directions on How to Say the Rosary:
Sign of the Cross
Apostles Creed
Our Father
3 Hail Mary's
Glory Be
1st Mystery*
Our Father*
10 Hail Mary's*
Glory Be*
Hail, Holy Queen

(*Repeat for 2nd, 3rd, 4th, and 5th Mysteries)

Joyful Mysteries:
1. The Annunciation
2. The Visitation
3. The Birth of Jesus
4. The Presentation of Jesus
5. The Finding of the Child Jesus in the Temple

(When you are finished with the rosary, invite each student who wishes to follow the example of Mary and say "Yes" to God's call in their life to come forward and receive a carnation and an index card to take home with them. Remind them that these are signs of their commitment to God's call.)

Closing Prayer

Leader: Let us close in prayer.

Lord God, we come before you with an open heart. We come to say yes to the working of your will within our lives. Help us to have the courage and understanding to say yes to you.

We pray this in your name, our Lord, Jesus Christ.

All: Amen.

Leader: Let us go forth in the name of the Father and of the Son and of the Holy Spirit.

All: Amen.

Prayer Service
Site for Sore Eyes

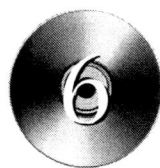

Preparation You will need the following items for this prayer service:
- Large wooden cross
- Large votive candle
- 4 taper candles
- Small flashlight (for scripture readings and leader sections)

Environment Set up the room with the large cross and the votive candle in the center of the room. Place the taper candles on either side of the votive candle. The room must be able to become completely dark. You will not want any light to be in the room with the exception of the votive candle. (Do not light the candle until instructed to do so.) Use black paper or fabric to block any residual light. Place all chairs in a circular rings surrounding the cross and candle.

Gathering Invite students to take a few moments to reflect upon the past couple of days—what has happened to them at school, at home, and in their activities. Give them a moment to quiet themselves and bring themselves into the presence of Christ.

Opening Prayer (Read in the front of the room, slowly and prayerfully.)

(stand)

Leader: We begin in the name of the Father and of the Son and of the Holy Spirit. Amen.

Heavenly Father, we sit in total darkness, anxious for you to enlighten our lives. We thank you for bringing us together today so we may grow closer to you. Help us in our journey to be mindful of your love and compassion even during the times we cannot see it. Send your Holy Spirit to walk with us as we discover your fire within our souls. Lord Jesus, you are the light that breaks the darkness. *(brief pause)*

(Light the votive candle.)

Leader: Lord Jesus, we know you are only a prayer away from us. May we light your fire within our prayer lives and build upon our relationship with you. *(brief pause)*

(Light the first taper candle.)

Leader: Christ Jesus, you ask us to be reconciled with our neighbors and ourselves. May we light your fire within our need for this forgiveness. *(brief pause)*

(Light the second taper candle.)

Leader: Lord Jesus, your presence stretches from the mountains to the prairies, across the oceans and the seas. May we light your fire within your presence in our lives. *(brief pause)*

(Light the third taper candle.)

Leader: Heavenly Father, the fire of your love burns within us. May we light your fire of love within our daily lives so we may accept the freedom that only you can provide. *(brief pause)*

(Light the fourth taper candle.)

(Play the song "Site for Sore Eyes.")

(sit)

Readings

Reader: A reading from the Gospel according to Matthew. (Matthew 28:16–20)

All: Glory to you, O Lord.

Reader: The eleven disciples went to Galilee, to the mountain to which Jesus had ordered them. When they saw him, they worshiped, but they doubted. Then Jesus approached and said to them, "All power in heaven and on earth has been given to me. Go, therefore, and make disciples of all nations, baptizing them in the name of the Father, and of the Son, and of the Holy Spirit, teaching them to observe all that I have commanded you. And behold, I am with you always, until the end of the age."

The Gospel of the Lord.

All: Praise to you, Lord Jesus Christ.

Reflection

(A short reflection should be given by the leader or another appropriate person on how Jesus is the "site for their sore eyes.")

Leader: Reflect for a moment on all the areas of your life Jesus has touched.

In a moment, we will ask you to prayerfully share in 5 words or less the area Christ has touched in your life that you feel is the most important.

(Take the large votive candle and hold it.)

Leader: Lord Jesus, you are the site for our sore eyes. You are the fire that burns within our soul. You are the one who sets us free from our sins. You have touched our lives, and we are truly thankful for your presence. In prayerful thanksgiving, we recognize the times or areas of our lives that you have impacted. I invite you to come forward, one at a time, and take the light of Christ as you share.

(Share your area/time and then pass the candle to a participant. More candles should be lit if the room is too dark to walk in safely. Do not use the lights.)

Closing Prayer

(Once finished, close with a prayer of thanksgiving for the gifts that Christ blesses us with, especially the gift of life. Also include thanksgiving for all the areas in our life that Jesus has touched.)

Leader: Let us go forth in the name of the Father and of the Son and of the Holy Spirit.

All: Amen.

PRAYER SERVICE

His Life

Preparation   You will need the following items for this prayer service:
- Large wooden cross (at least 4 feet tall)
- White ribbons, 12–18 inches long (1 per participant)
- Blue markers (for writing on the ribbons)

Environment   Set up the room with the cross in the front of the room. Place the ribbons and markers at the foot of the cross. If chairs are desired, place them in half circles facing the cross.

Gathering   Invite students to take a few moments to reflect upon the past couple of days—what has happened to them at school, at home, and in their activities. Give them a moment to quiet themselves and bring themselves into the presence of Christ.

Opening Prayer   (Read in the front of the room, slowly and prayerfully.)

(stand)

Leader: We begin in the name of the Father and of the Son and of the Holy Spirit. Amen.

Father, we thank you for this opportunity to gather and celebrate our belief in you. We thank you for sacrificing so much for us sinners. We ask that you open our eyes to see the way that our lives are affected by the choices we make. Help us to make the proper choices that will influence our lives in a positive way. We ask this in your name, our Lord Jesus Christ.

All: Amen.

Leader: We take a moment to remember the times we have failed to follow Christ.

You forgive our failings in the choices we make. Lord, have mercy.

All: Lord, have mercy.

Prayer Services

Leader: You call us to live holy and blessed lives. Christ, have mercy.

All: Christ, have mercy.

Leader: You call us to walk the narrow path of your teachings. Lord, have mercy.

All: Lord, have mercy.

Leader: May almighty God bless us and protect us from all evil.

All: Amen.

(sit)

Readings

Reader: A reading from the Gospel according to Luke. (Luke 9:18–27)

All: Glory to you, O Lord.

Reader: Once when Jesus was praying in solitude, and the disciples were with him, he asked them, "Who do the crowds say that I am?" They said in reply, "John the Baptist; others, Elijah; still others, 'One of the ancient prophets has arisen.'" Then he said to them, "But who do you say that I am?" Peter said in reply, "The Messiah of God." He rebuked them and directed them not to tell this to anyone. He said, "The Son of Man must suffer greatly and be rejected by the elders, the chief priests, and the scribes, and be killed and on the third day be raised." Then he said to all, "If anyone wishes to come after me, he must deny himself and take up his cross daily and follow me. For whoever wishes to save his life will lose it, but whoever loses his life for my sake will save it. What profit is there for one to gain the whole world yet lose or forfeit himself? Whoever is ashamed of me and of my words, the Son of Man will be ashamed of when he comes in his glory and in the glory of the Father and of the holy angels. Truly I say to you, there are some standing here who will not taste death until they see the kingdom of God."

The Gospel of the Lord.

All: Praise to you, Lord Jesus Christ.

Fall on Your Knees · His Life

Reflection

Leader: Take a moment to reflect on the choices you have made in your life.

What choices would you change? What choices would you strengthen?

(pause)

Leader: Listen to the song "His Life." What does this song say about the choices you have made in your life? What does it say about what Christ did for you?

(Play the song "His Life.")

Leader: Christ died on the cross for us so we may be saved from the sinful choices we make.

Our sins were carried with Christ to his crucifixion. Our sins were then nailed to the cross with Christ. As Jesus conquered death, he also conquered all of our sins. We lift up our hearts in thanksgiving for his precious gift.

As we listen to the song "His Life" once again, we invite you to come forward one at a time and write your name on one of the ribbons. Then tie the ribbon to the cross as a symbol of your thankfulness to Christ.

(Play the song "His Life" again.)

Closing Prayer

(Once everyone is finished, invite students to encircle the cross. Then close with the Lord's Prayer.)

Leader: Let us go forth in the name of the Father and of the Son and of the Holy Spirit.

All: Amen.

Prayer Service

Wish

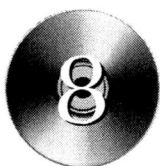

Preparation You will need the following items for this prayer service:
- Large wooden cross (at least 4 feet tall)
- Large votive candle
- Small sheets of colored paper and a writing utensil (1 each per person)
- Small sheets of white paper (1 per person)
- Basket
- Tape

Environment Set up the room with the cross and the votive candle placed in the middle. If chairs are desired, have them encircle the cross. As each participant enters the room, have them take a sheet of the colored paper and a writing utensil. Ask them to write down in 10 words or less what the word "love" means to them. Collect and preview all of the participants' answers. Scatter the answers around the foot of the cross.

Gathering Invite students to take a few moments to reflect upon the past couple of days—what has happened to them at school, at home, and in their activities. Give them a moment to quiet themselves and bring themselves into the presence of Christ.

Opening Prayer (Read in the front of the room, slowly and prayerfully.)

(stand)

Leader: We begin in the name of the Father and of the Son and of the Holy Spirit. Amen.

Good and gracious God, we thank you for this day. We also thank you for blessing us with your love. Through your love, we are given forgiveness and comfort. It is with your love that we experience hope, joy, and happiness. Help us to imitate your love in our relationships with others. Teach us the importance of loving one another. Most importantly, show us how to love like you. We ask this in your name, Lord Jesus Christ.

Prayer Services

All: Amen.

(sit)

Readings

(Ask 2 readers to come forward and share each of the following scripture verses.)

Reader 1: 1 Corinthians 13:4–13
Love is patient, love is kind. It is not jealous, [love] is not pompous, it is not inflated, it is not rude, it does not seek its own interests, it is not quick-tempered, it does not brood over injury, it does not rejoice over wrongdoing but rejoices with the truth. It bears all things, believes all things, hopes all things, endures all things. Love never fails. If there are prophecies, they will be brought to nothing; if tongues, they will cease; if knowledge, it will be brought to nothing. For we know partially and we prophesy partially, but when the perfect comes, the partial will pass away. When I was a child, I used to talk as a child, think as a child, reason as a child; when I became a man, I put aside childish things. At present we see indistinctly, as in a mirror, but then face to face. At present I know partially; then I shall know fully, as I am fully known. So faith, hope, love remain, these three; but the greatest of these is love.

Reader 2: John 3:16–21
For God so loved the world that he gave his only Son, so that everyone who believes in him might not perish but might have eternal life. For God did not send his Son into the world to condemn the world, but that the world might be saved through him. Whoever believes in him will not be condemned, but whoever does not believe has already been condemned, because he has not believed in the name of the only Son of God.

Leader: This is what scripture tells us about love. What is it that you say about love?

(Invite 1 participant at a time to walk up to the cross and randomly pick up one of the sheets of paper to read to the rest of the group. Do this until all sheets have been read or 5 minutes have passed, whichever comes first. You do not want to drag this part on too long. After each answer is read, tape the sheet of paper to the floor, forming a heart around the base of the cross.)

Reflection

Leader: Christ promises us that he loves us so much that he is always by our side. The song "Wish" focuses on the importance of standing by the side of a person you love. As we listen to the song, let us reflect upon our relationships with others—how we stand by their side as Christ stands by us, how we love as Christ loved, how we live the many definitions of love.

(Play the song "Wish." When finished, hand out the sheets of white paper. Ask the participants to write a personal prayer intention based on their desire to love as Christ loved. Place the basket within the heart that was created with the definitions of love. Ask the participants to place their completed intentions in the basket.)

Closing Prayer

Leader: Let us pray. Heavenly Father, we place our intentions before you. Please listen to our prayers and answer them according to your will.

(Encourage each participant to walk to the basket and randomly select one of the intentions. Have each participant read the intention aloud in a prayerful manner, and then tape it on top of one of the pieces of paper that form the heart around the cross.)

Leader: Good and gracious Father, your love for us surrounds the prayers we have placed before you. Grant us peace in our hearts and joy in our relationships. We ask this in your name, Lord Jesus Christ.

All: Amen.

Leader: Let us go forth in the name of the Father and of the Son and of the Holy Spirit.

All: Amen.

Prayer Service

Praise

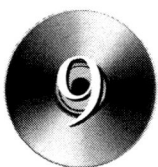

Preparation You will need the following items for this prayer service:
- Large wooden cross
- Large glass bowl filled with Holy Water
- Candles
- Palms (or similar plants)
- Small pedestal table (about waist high)

(Note: If possible, have your pastor or another priest present for this prayer service to bless the Holy Water during the Opening Prayer. If no one is available, the water will need to be blessed prior to the service.)

Environment Place the large cross in the front of the room with the large bowl of Holy Water on a small pedestal table in front of the cross. Place the candles on either side of the cross. The palms or plants should be placed adjacent to the bowl of water to give it a "natural" feel.

Gathering Invite students to take a few moments to reflect upon the past couple of days—what has happened to them at school, at home, and in their activities. Give them a moment to quiet themselves and bring themselves into the presence of Christ.

Opening Prayer (Read in the front of the room, slowly and prayerfully.)

(stand)

Leader: We begin in the name of the Father and of the Son and of the Holy Spirit. Amen.

Lord Jesus Christ, you came to walk among us. You were sent by your Father to teach us and to guide us. Today we offer our time to you in thanksgiving and praise. We give you the glory that you desire. We give you the praise that you deserve. As humble servants, we raise our eyes to you in search of peace. Open our ears that we may hear your word. Open our eyes that we may see your way. Open our hearts that we may know your love. And open our souls that we may live like you. You have called us through our baptism. Therefore, through the reminder of our baptism, we thank you and give all glory and praise to you. We ask this in your name, our Lord Jesus Christ.

All: Amen.

(Invite the participants to gather around the bowl of Holy Water. If a priest is available, have the priest bless the water once everyone is gathered around.)

Leader: Take a moment to think about all the uses we have for water. *(pause)*

It is used for cleaning. It is used for purification. It is used for entertainment. Mostly, though, it is used for life. We all know we cannot survive very long without water. It must be a part of our everyday life. In this same way, we cannot survive without our faith. Our faith must be a part of our everyday life. Water reminds us of our faith. Water reminds us of our baptism. In baptism we are cleansed and we are purified. Today we remind ourselves of our baptism.

Readings

Reader: In those days, John the Baptist appeared, preaching in the desert of Judea saying, "Repent, for the kingdom of heaven is at hand!" It was of him that the prophet Isaiah had spoken when he said, "A voice of one crying out in the desert, 'Prepare the way of the Lord, make straight his paths.'" John wore clothing made of camel's hair and had a leather belt around his waist. His food was locusts and wild honey. At that time, Jerusalem, all Judea, and the whole region around the Jordan were going out to him and were being baptized by him in the Jordan River as they acknowledged their sins. When he saw many of the Pharisees and Sadducees coming to his baptism, he said to them, "You brood of vipers! Who warned you to flee from the coming wrath? Produce good fruit as evidence of your repentance. And do not presume to say to yourselves, 'We have Abraham as our father.' For I tell you, God can raise up children to Abraham from these stones. Even now the ax lies at the root of the trees. Therefore, every tree that does not bear good fruit will be cut down and thrown into the fire.

I am baptizing you with water, for repentance, but the one who is coming after me is mightier than I. I am not worthy to carry his sandals. He will baptize you with the holy Spirit and fire.

His winnowing fan is in his hand. He will clear his threshing floor and gather his wheat into his barn, but the chaff he will burn with unquenchable fire." Then Jesus came from Galilee to John at the Jordan to be baptized by him. John tried to prevent him, saying, "I need to be baptized by you, and yet you are coming to me?" Jesus said to him in reply, "Allow it now, for thus it is fitting for us to fulfill all righteousness." Then he allowed him.

After Jesus was baptized, he came up from the water, and behold, the heavens were opened, and he saw the Spirit of God descending like a dove and coming upon him. And a voice came from the heavens, saying, "This is my beloved Son, with whom I am well pleased."

The Gospel of the Lord.

All: Praise to you, Lord Jesus Christ.

Reflection

(A short reflection by the prayer service leader on the gospel reading is encouraged prior to continuing with the rest of the service.)

Leader: Let us take a moment to think about what our baptism means to us.

Are we thankful for the gifts that have been given to us?
Do we strive to improve our lives and live as Christ has taught us to live?
Do we give all praise and glory to our God?

Meditate on these questions as we listen to the words of the song "Praise."

(Play the song "Praise.")

Leader: We are called by our baptism to live a Christian lifestyle. So let us pray...

All: *(recite the Lord's Prayer)*

Leader: When Jesus appeared to his disciples, he said, "Peace be with you." So in turn, we say to each other, "Peace be with you." This water reminds us that we are one body in Christ through our baptism. As that one body, we must encourage each other to live the Christian life and to share the good news of our Lord Jesus Christ with all those who we come in contact with.

Let us share a sign of Christ's peace with each other.

Closing Prayer

Leader: Let us pray. Holy and gracious God, you do not need praise and glory from us, but in our actions may our praise and glory be a gift to you. We thank you for the many gifts you give to us. We thank you for the happiness and the challenges that are in our daily lives. Help us to always remember the purpose of our baptism. May we always be good stewards of our gifts and live the life you want us to live. We ask this in your name, our personal savior, our Lord Jesus Christ.

All: Amen.

Leader: Let us go forth in the name of the Father and of the Son and of the Holy Spirit.

All: Amen.

Prayer Service
Nails That Pierced

Preparation You will need the following items for this prayer service:
- Large wooden cross (at least 4 feet tall)
- Several large votive candles
- Purple fabric
- Small sheets of flash paper (can be purchased at a theatre supply store)
- Long candle
- Large clay bowl (for burning the flash paper)
- Priests to administer the Sacrament of Reconciliation
- Soft music (for Reconciliation)

(Caution: Flash paper burns very quickly without leaving much ash. Be careful when igniting the bowl of intentions. You may want to experiment with a few pieces of flash paper first before doing this prayer service. Also, do not ignite the flash paper indoors unless in a very safe location. It is also advised to have a fire extinguisher nearby.)

Environment Set up the room with the large cross in the front of the room. Wrap the base of the cross with the purple cloth. Place the large votive candles on stands to the right and left of the cross. Place the clay bowl on the foot of the cross.

Gathering Invite students to take a few moments to reflect upon the past couple of days—what has happened to them at school, at home, and in their activities. Give them a moment to quiet themselves and bring themselves into the presence of Christ.

Opening Prayer (Read in the front of the room, slowly and prayerfully.)

(stand)

Leader: We begin in the name of the Father and of the Son and of the Holy Spirit. Amen.

Prayer Services

Heavenly Father, we come before you today as a broken people. Our hearts yearn for the peace only you can provide. Only you can lift the weight from our soul. Be with us today as we seek your forgiveness. We ask this in your name, our Lord, Jesus Christ.

All: Amen.

Readings

Reader: A reading from the Gospel according to Luke. (Luke 23:1–46)

All: Glory to you, O Lord.

Reader: Then the whole assembly of them arose and brought him before Pilate. They brought charges against him, saying, "We found this man misleading our people; he opposes the payment of taxes to Caesar and maintains that he is the Messiah, a king." Pilate asked him, "Are you the king of the Jews?" He said to him in reply, "You say so." Pilate then addressed the chief priests and the crowds, "I find this man not guilty." But they were adamant and said, "He is inciting the people with his teaching throughout all Judea, from Galilee where he began even to here."

On hearing this, Pilate asked if the man was a Galilean; and upon learning that he was under Herod's jurisdiction, he sent him to Herod who was in Jerusalem at that time. Herod was very glad to see Jesus; he had been wanting to see him for a long time, for he had heard about him and had been hoping to see him perform some sign. He questioned him at length, but he gave him no answer. The chief priests and scribes, meanwhile, stood by accusing him harshly. [Even] Herod and his soldiers treated him contemptuously and mocked him, and after clothing him in resplendent garb, he sent him back to Pilate. Herod and Pilate became friends that very day, even though they had been enemies formerly. Pilate then summoned the chief priests, the rulers, and the people and said to them, "You brought this man to me and accused him of inciting the people to revolt. I have conducted my investigation in your presence and have not found this man guilty of the charges you have brought against him, nor did Herod, for he sent him back to us. So no capital crime has been committed by him. Therefore, I shall have him flogged and then release him."

But all together they shouted out, "Away with this man! Release Barabbas to us." (Now Barabbas had been imprisoned for a rebellion that had taken place in the city and for murder.) Again Pilate addressed them, still wishing to release Jesus, but they continued their shouting, "Crucify him! Crucify him!" Pilate addressed them a third time, "What evil has this man done? I found him guilty of no capital crime. Therefore, I shall have him flogged and then release him." With loud shouts, however, they persisted in calling for his crucifixion, and their voices prevailed. The verdict of Pilate was that their demand should be granted. So he released the man who had been imprisoned for rebellion and murder, for whom they asked, and he handed Jesus over to them to deal with as they wished.

As they led him away, they took hold of a certain Simon, a Cyrenian, who was coming in from the country; and after laying the cross on him, they made him carry it behind Jesus. A large crowd of people followed Jesus, including many women who mourned and lamented him. Jesus turned to them and said, "Daughters of Jerusalem, do not weep for me; weep instead for yourselves and for your children, for indeed, the days are coming when people will say, 'Blessed are the barren, the wombs that never bore and the breasts that never nursed.' At that time people will say to the mountains, 'Fall upon us!' and to the hills, 'Cover us!' for if these things are done when the wood is green, what will happen when it is dry?" Now two others, both criminals, were led away with him to be executed. When they came to the place called the Skull, they crucified him and the criminals there, one on his right, the other on his left. (Then Jesus said, "Father, forgive them, they know not what they do.") They divided his garments by casting lots. The people stood by and watched; the rulers, meanwhile, sneered at him and said, "He saved others, let him save himself if he is the chosen one, the Messiah of God." Even the soldiers jeered at him. As they approached to offer him wine they called out, "If you are King of the Jews, save yourself." Above him, there was an inscription that read, "This is the King of the Jews."

Now one of the criminals hanging there reviled Jesus, saying, "Are you not the Messiah? Save yourself and us." The other, however, rebuking him, said in reply, "Have you no fear of God, for you are subject to the same condemnation? And indeed, we have been condemned justly, for the sentence we received corresponds to our crimes, but this man has done nothing criminal." Then he said, "Jesus, remember me when you come into your kingdom." He replied to him, "Amen, I say to you, today you will be with me in Paradise."

It was now about noon and darkness came over the whole land until three in the afternoon because of an eclipse of the sun. Then the veil of the temple was torn down the middle. Jesus cried out in a loud voice, "Father, into your hands I commend my spirit"; and when he had said this, he breathed his last.

The Gospel of the Lord.

All: Praise to you, Lord Jesus Christ.

(sit)

Reflection

Leader: Take a moment and picture in your minds the scene portrayed by this Gospel. What do you see? Think of the criminals crucified on the right and left sides of Jesus. Think of Jesus' mother at the foot of the cross. Picture the nails in Christ's wrists and in his feet. (pause)

He died for you and I. He died so we might have life. He died so our sins would be forgiven. Quietly in our hearts, let us reflect upon the recent times in our life when we have failed. When have we turned away from Christ to satisfy our earthly desires? Recall the times when we have not lived by our Christian faith.

(stand)

All: I confess to you, almighty God, and to you, my brothers and sisters, that I have sinned through my own fault. In my thoughts and in my words, in what I have done and what I have failed to do. And I ask the Blessed Mary, ever Virgin, all the angels and saints, and you, my brothers and sisters, to pray for me to the Lord our God.

(sit)

(Play the song "Nails That Pierced.")

Leader: We invite you to receive the Sacrament of Reconciliation.

(Give directions as to where the priests will be stationed.)

Fall on Your Knees · Nails That Pierced

Leader: After you have received the Sacrament and after you have completed your penance, come forward and take a piece of the flash paper. Write on it, "Lord, I thank you for forgiveness," and sign your name. Fold the paper in half and place it in the bowl. Then return to your seat until all confessions have been heard.

(Play soft background music while the Sacrament is administered. When all confessions are complete and everyone has placed their flash paper in the bowl, have someone light the long candle from one of the votive candles. Proceed with all of the participants to go outside or to a location where the bowl can be ignited safely.)

Leader: Christ grants us peace by forgiving our sins. Let us pray in thanksgiving for this peace.

All: (recite the Lord's Prayer)

Closing Prayer

Leader: Father, we thank you for answering our prayers and forgiving us our sins. Take our sins from us, for you have promised us that you forgive and forget. May we always strive to live our lives as you have asked us to. We ask for your guidance. In your name, Lord Jesus Christ.

All: Amen.

Leader: Let us go forth in the name of the Father and of the Son and of the Holy Spirit.

All: Amen.

(Light the bowl with the long candle.)

Prayer Service
This Is Your Choice

Preparation

You will need the following items for this prayer service:
- Large wooden cross (at least 4 feet tall)
- Large votive candle
- Brown paper bags (lunch size)
- Tape
- Marker

Prepare the participants in advance of this session by asking them to bring something that symbolizes a bad choice they have made in their recent past. Be sure to tell them that this will be confidential and that no one will see what object they bring. The object must fit in a brown paper bag. When participants arrive, give them one of the bags and ask them to place their object inside, fold over the top of the bag, and tape it shut. Have them write their name on the top. They should then place the bag around the foot of the cross.

Environment

Set up the room with the cross and the votive candle in the center. If chairs are desired, they should encircle the cross and candle. Leave enough room to place all of the bags at the foot of the cross and still be able to walk around the cross.

Gathering

Invite students to take a few moments to reflect upon the past couple of days—what has happened to them at school, at home, and in their activities. Give them a moment to quiet themselves and bring themselves into the presence of Christ.

Opening Prayer

(Read in the front of the room, slowly and prayerfully.)

(stand)

Leader: We begin in the name of the Father and of the Son and of the Holy Spirit. Amen.

Lord Jesus, we come before you today with open hearts. We come before you with the desire to improve our lives and strengthen our relationship with you. We place at the foot of your cross our struggles, our sins, and our crosses. Challenge us, Lord, to follow in your ways. We ask this in your name, our Lord Jesus Christ.

All: Amen.

Readings

Reader: A reading from the Gospel according to John. (John 8:2–11)

All: Glory to you, O Lord.

Reader: But early in the morning he arrived again in the temple area, and all the people started coming to him, and he sat down and taught them. Then the scribes and the Pharisees brought a woman who had been caught in adultery and made her stand in the middle. They said to him, "Teacher, this woman was caught in the very act of committing adultery. Now in the law, Moses commanded us to stone such women. So what do you say?" They said this to test him, so they could have some charge to bring against him. Jesus bent down and began to write on the ground with his finger. But when they continued asking him, he straightened up and said to them, "Let the one among you who is without sin be the first to throw a stone at her."

Again he bent down and wrote on the ground. And in response, they went away one by one, beginning with the elders. So he was left alone with the woman before him. Then Jesus straightened up and said to her, "Woman, where are they? Has no one condemned you?" She replied, "No one, sir." Then Jesus said, "Neither do I condemn you. Go, [and] from now on do not sin any more."

The Gospel of the Lord.

All: Praise to you, Lord Jesus Christ.

(sit)

Reflection

(Play the song "This Is Your Choice")

Leader: These paper bags represent our choices. We place them at the foot of the cross as a request to Christ to help us overcome these challenges in our lives. Everything in life is a choice. As Christians, we are called to turn away from our sinful choices. Like the woman caught in adultery in John's Gospel, we are forgiven by Christ but called to never repeat the sin. This is the cross we bear every day. This is the choice we must make every day. We decide for ourselves that Jesus Christ is the way. So together with our Holy Mother, we pray.

(Alternate boys and girls, or split the group into two. After each prayer, recite a Hail Mary.)

Girls: We pray for humility as we bear our crosses every day.

Boys: We pray for strength to say "no" to the things that pull us away from you, Lord.

Girls: We pray for the wisdom to know what is right, holy, and true.

Boys: We pray for patience in our struggles to follow our Savior, Jesus Christ.

Girls: We pray for hope in our quest to choose the right path.

Boys: We pray for courage in the times when we are challenged by our friends and peers.

Girls: We pray for reconciliation with all persons we have hurt by our choices.

Boys: We pray for our salvation through the grace of our Lord, Jesus Christ.

Leader: We ask all this in your name, our Lord, Jesus Christ.

All: Amen.

(Encourage participants to retrieve their brown bag from the foot of the cross.)

Closing Prayer

Leader: Let us close in prayer.

Lord Jesus, we thank you for your never-ceasing love. Please continue to guide us in the daily choices that we face. Help us to make the right choice that leads us closer to you.

We ask this in your name, our Lord, Jesus Christ.

All: Amen.

Leader: Let us go forth in the name of the Father and of the Son and of the Holy Spirit.

All: Amen.